Emotional Lives

Emotional Lives explores the changes in *emotional cultures* that have taken place during the last half century and continue to affect people's identities today. These changes are driven by the culture of consumerism in contemporary postindustrial society and by the emergence of new ideas about public and private life in a time when media culture generates new forms of social relationships and deep personal attachments to celebrity figures. McCarthy shows that people are drawn to public life, not only for entertainment and pleasure but also for its dramas, for memorializing events like disasters, acts of violence, and victimhood. McCarthy's cultural-sociological approach provides new insights about emotions as "social things" and reveals how today mass media is an important force for cultural change, including changes in people's relationships, identities, and emotions.

E. DOYLE MCCARTHY is Professor of Sociology and American Studies at Fordham University in New York. She has worked and published in the fields of sociology of knowledge and emotion studies. She serves on the editorial board of *La Critica Sociologia*, an international journal in the social sciences; previously she was senior editor of the *International Journal of Politics, Culture, and Society*, was elected chair of the Emotions Section of the American Sociological Association, and served on the executive committee of the International Society for Research on Emotions (ISRE) from 2004 to 2007.

STUDIES IN EMOTION AND SOCIAL INTERACTION
Second Series

Series Editors
Keith Oatley
University of Toronto

Antony S. R. Manstead
Cardiff University

(*Continued after Index*)

Emotional Lives

Dramas of Identity in an Age of Mass Media

E. DOYLE MCCARTHY

Fordham University

CAMBRIDGE
UNIVERSITY PRESS

CAMBRIDGE
UNIVERSITY PRESS

University Printing House, Cambridge CB2 8BS, United Kingdom

One Liberty Plaza, 20th Floor, New York, NY 10006, USA

477 Williamstown Road, Port Melbourne, VIC 3207, Australia

4843/24, 2nd Floor, Ansari Road, Daryaganj, Delhi – 110002, India

79 Anson Road, #06–04/06, Singapore 079906

Cambridge University Press is part of the University of Cambridge.

It furthers the University's mission by disseminating knowledge in the pursuit of education, learning, and research at the highest international levels of excellence.

www.cambridge.org
Information on this title: www.cambridge.org/9780521820141
DOI: 10.1017/9781139028844

First published 2017

A catalogue record for this publication is available from the British Library.

ISBN 978-0-521-82014-1 Hardback

For
JJH

Contents

Acknowledgments

I am thankful to those who took the time to read the book's chapters and who gave me many helpful comments and critical commentaries: David D. Franks, Guy Oakes, Robert S. Perinbanayagam, and Marvin Scott.

Keith Oatley, one of the book's Series Editors, provided valuable advice and criticism as well as consistent support throughout the extended period of research and writing. Without that continued support the project would have been much more difficult to complete.

Special thanks are due to my friends and colleagues in the Society for the Study of Symbolic Interaction (SSSI), the International Society for Research on Emotions (ISRE), and the Sociology of Emotions section of the American Sociological Association. These organizations each provided both a social arena and a most hospitable and collegial environment for testing my thinking and my ongoing work in emotion studies.

I would like to thank Dean John Harrington for his support of a Faculty Fellowship leave in Fall 2013 and for the opportunity to apply for research funds for the book index. Thanks, too, to Professor Allan Gilbert, chair of my department (2008–14) at Fordham, who supported me throughout this extended project of research and writing. Professor Hugo Benavides, my current chair, is also due my thanks for his interest and support of me and my work.

On a rainy weekend in June 2005, Captain Dan Gillespie and my cousin Polly Gillespie graciously offered me their home in Washington, DC, and guided me on a tour of the Holocaust Museum, Washington's war memorials, and Arlington National Cemetery. This memorable visit and our conversations were the beginning of and the inspiration for my work on chapter 3.

David Franks and Audrey Franks provided continued and valuable friendship and support throughout this writing project and offered many important insights on social theory and emotion studies. Years ago, before there was a field called the sociology of emotions, David invited me to begin work with him in emotions studies. We have shared many happy years of intense collaboration working on the study of emotions.

Some colleagues and friends provided valuable ideas and exchanges that became important to my thinking and writing about emotions: Franco Ferrarotti, Eva Illouz, Angela Zanotti, Emma Engdahl, Edward T. Linenthal, George Ritzer, Thomas Scheff, Norman K. Denzin, Ira J. Cohen, Donileen Loseke, David Altheide, Norman Denzin, Carolyn Ellis, and Lauren Langman.

Stephanie Laudone worked with me in 2013 on a paper and conference presentations on mass media and human suffering. Michelle Rufrano collaborated with me in 2015–16 on papers and presentations on mass media and collective emotions. Thanks to each of you for our exchanges and our work together.

Hetty Marx and Janka Romero, editors at Cambridge University Press, assisted me in bringing this project to completion and into print.

An early version of chapter 1, on constructionist theories of emotions, appeared in the journal *Social Perspectives on Emotions*, volume 2, edited by William M. Wentworth, under the title "The Social Construction of Emotions," pp. 267–78.

An early version of chapter 3 on memorializing appeared in the volume *Authenticity in Culture, Self, and Society*. Thanks to its editors, Phillip Vannini and Patrick Williams, for allowing me to begin my work with their invaluable support.

Preface

Drama as Everyday Experience

Years ago, Raymond Williams argued that our postmodern lives had in effect turned us into actors. In fact, we may be distinguished from all known human societies in the sheer amount of acting that we observe on a day-to-day basis. What we have now is "drama as habitual experience" (R. Williams [1974] 1989, 3–5). The long tradition of performance theory in the social sciences draws from and systematizes this postmodern everyday experience, making mass media and the audience the social arena where the meaning of a performance is created and where social actors "encounter their identities" and those of others (Giesen 2006; cf. Gross 1986; Schechner 2003; Turner 1988).

This book is an attempt to understand the many ways that our everyday theatricality has shaped our feelings and emotions *and* (as dialectical thinking requires) to consider how our feelings and emotions move us along a new social trajectory that seeks out dramatic experiences as ways of discovering reality itself. I also want to provide here a kind of record of the many shapes and forms of these emotional dramas: the ones we are used to viewing on the digital screens we watch and inhabit; the dramas we ourselves enact in shopping malls and public parks; the horrific events we see and consume as *the news* day after day, and the dramas enacted by those heroes who play leading parts and dangerous roles, like cops and firemen; the rock concerts and football games we attend as fans and participants; the museums and monuments we enter as participants in an unfolding drama.

When "real people" describe themselves in public settings like these, their speech sometimes reveals their sense of something real and emotional, even life-affirming, happening to them in these public places, suggesting that "authenticity" has become a vital cultural code (Alexander and Mast 2006), personally meaningful to each of us and important in the signs we give off to others, a code used and pursued by social actors in public places in an age of artifice, drama, and manipulation. So it is that visitors to memorials, for example, engage in public acts with others, becoming part of the montage they visit, participants in a "spectacle of suffering," members of an "imagined bereaved community" (Linenthal 2001, 2–3).

While Lionel Trilling (1971) first pointed out to us the literary and cultural significance of "authenticity" in our time, Alexander and Mast (2006, 2) first described *social performances* like those described above as dramas of "authenticity," referring to the growing number of intense and emotional social performances today and to the fact that, increasingly, dramas are built into the rhythms of our everyday lives, where social actors across a range of public venues implicitly position themselves and their actions on a public stage, "seeking identification with their experiences and understandings from their audiences."

As I argue here, collective acts like these suggest that a new postmodern social imaginary may be at work today, one only decades old. Earlier in this long history, modernity famously inserted distance between human subjects, a *rational* distance (as Max Weber called it) of separation and restraint. It was also a personal distance—we had become strangers to ourselves—one that Freud described and invited us moderns to overcome. Is this distance being replaced today by one for *closeness*—a closeness between subjects, between our private and our public selves? Can this closeness help us understand today's newfound urgency to feel things firsthand and for a new desire to enter public spaces (Kimmelman 2016)? If this is so, collective acts like those I describe here operate as signs of a new phase of modern subjectivity, a new "social imaginary," one described by Daniel Bell (1996) as the "eclipse of distance." This is one of my arguments in the chapters that follow.

Borrowing from authors working in culture theory (chapter 1), I examine what a cultural approach to emotions looks like and what it

studies. As I argue here, its approach takes up the question of modern
and postmodern identity (chapter 2) and how emotions have been
experienced and interpreted by social actors living today. I also argue,
with the help of social theorists and social historians, that today's
emotional experiences and dramas have their roots in earlier
emotional cultures, especially the social movement described as
Romanticism. Accordingly, my approach to identity and emotional
life is historical, arguing that important changes have taken place
throughout the modern era in people's ideas of the self and in the
emotions people feel, and what emotions mean to them and to their
identities.

In chapter 2, I examine how emotions and identity—how people
come to think about who they are and who they want to be—have
become closely implicated in each other's careers as what we call
modernity has moved and changed into what we now call
postmodernity—that world of today where consumerism has taken off
at great speed and where consumerism's partner, mass media, spawns
an extraordinary thing called "celebrity culture," where people called
celebrities are known for being known or famous for being famous
(Boorstin 1961; Muggeridge 1967). Postmodernity is also a place where
its celebrities and its spectacles seem to be what many of us live for or,
at the very least, look to for our greatest source of relief from our
pedestrian lives.

Chapter 3 addresses a particular case of today's mediatized
world: the rise of memorials to death and disaster where the disaster
memorial (in the wake of plane crashes, street killings, school
shootings, and other familiar events of death and disaster) provides
a type of stage where numbers of us can enter and discover the
liberating experiences and the deep feelings of remembering events we
never witnessed directly but have come to know and to feel as our
very own.

Chapter 4 examines some of the ways that our emotional lives
have been altered in and through forms of mass media. The social
movements discussed in this chapter share an emotional intensity and

a consciousness of belonging to a large group of others like ourselves, whether the enthusiastic followers of a young Catholic saint, or the crowds dancing in the streets after Lindbergh's landing in Paris, or the vast and consequential community we call *the nation*. These collective unities—some lasting, some fleeting—are made up of beings who share a faith and/or an identity as *individuals* (discussed in chapter 2) with a common object, a mass of individuals united in time and space whose individualities merge in a moment of belonging to and participating in an idea and image of themselves—an idea communicated to them on television and in newspapers. Today these messages and images come to us on the many screens that surround us or are carried in our hands or pockets.

In the Afterword, I conclude this work on a personal note about what it has meant to try to study emotions today.

I Cultural Sociology and the Study of Emotions

> *"Structure of feeling* ... is the culture of a period: it is the particular living result of all the elements in the general organization ... I do not mean that the structure of feeling, any more than the social character, is possessed in the same way by the many individuals in the community. But I think it is a very deep and very wide possession, in all actual communities, precisely because it is on it that communication depends."
>
> Raymond Williams (1961, 48)

The notion "structure of feeling" was developed by Raymond Williams to give an account of people's responses to changes they were undergoing in English society since the eighteenth century. This was, in fact, a period of "decisive change" in almost all of social life, in literature and painting, in industry and engineering, in new conventions and institutions. People's creative activities, he argued, especially in the beginning of the nineteenth century, included far more than art, embracing "miracles" of human creative skill found in industry and engineering. "These are our poems," Thomas Carlyle said in 1842, looking at one of the new steam locomotives (R. Williams 1961, 71; cf. Emerson and Emerson, 1909). So, for example, Williams places the locomotive engine as central to the entire culture of the early- to mid-nineteenth century, a fact so important to the time and so often overlooked since then.

In this chapter and the following, like Williams, I intend to show that in our time, extraordinary creative forces of media and communication hold out to us a new and different structure of feeling from those of our predecessors living only a century ago, and only now becoming apparent to many of us. As Williams argued, this developing structure of feeling is our culture today. It is to be found in our most visible institutions—in our forms of mass media, in our forms of pleasure and entertainment, in the brute facts of our economy, in our forms of work, and in our social classes. But it is also discovered in our notions of community and nationhood, our beliefs in individuality and in family, and in the emotions we feel and those we seek out in our daily lives with others. It is in some of the new collective forms of public life and entertainment that I will seek out our very own structure of feeling: our Super Bowls and reality TV, our public displays of grief and mourning at sites of violence and human disaster, our political campaigns and conventions, our new forms of leisure like mountain climbing and movie tourism ("Put an Everest in your life!" or "Ride the streets of San Francisco with Bullitt!").

I will study emotions throughout as part of culture, a culture discovered in what we do as much as what we think, a culture that is deeply emotional and driven by the new forms of mass media and the environments media creates for us: an environment found on the many screens we incessantly watch and inhabit in our daily lives, the near-endless sounds and music we hear or are plugged into at our gyms, the digital conversations we hold with multiple others in our daily lives.

Long regarded as the province of psychologists, the study of emotions by sociologists was infrequent. Regarded as intruders, sociologists who studied emotions were violators of the rules of disciplinary segregation. This situation has changed considerably in recent decades as we have witnessed a number of disciplinary walls tumbling down and with that a "blurring" of academic genres. Today there is a new breed of "psychological anthropologists" as well as a good number of prominent philosophers writing about the emotions. As well, there are psychologists writing about "culture," and in my own field of sociology, the sociology of emotions continues to flourish and to take root in Europe after decades of research in the United States.[1]

The subject matter of the sociology of emotions is remarkably broad and diverse, covering studies that range from various group and institutional "cultures" of emotion to works on the role of emotions in the consumer economy. In this—its diversity of subject matter—the sociology of emotions reflects the direction that the discipline as a whole has taken for several decades. Once distinguished by a unitary theory and common set of assumptions, sociology has quickly become, in the relatively short span of a few decades, a field of diverse and conflicting approaches, while its purview has expanded to include fields as different as comparative historical studies and the phenomenology of everyday life. In many ways, the new diversity that has marked sociology for about four decades now has grown out of a movement of all the social sciences—economics, political science, and sociology—distinguished by a turn from a scientific to a more historical and critical stance to the study of societies and social change. This movement has also brought the study of culture to the forefront of these disciplines while advancing the interpretive approach to the study of human society and undermining the long-standing social-scientific claim to universal relevance and validity. Today, the various schools of social science have been formed relative to these controversies concerning culture's place in the social sciences, in particular whether or not the model for social-scientific inquiry is—as the culturalists would claim—language, the system and process for the study of representation, meaning, and interpretation (Rabinow and Sullivan [1979] 1987; Rabinow and Marcus 2008; Rabinow and Stavrianakis 2013).

Into this environment of change the sociology of emotions was introduced with early influential statements by Hochschild (1979; 1983), Heise (1977), Kemper (1978), Shott (1979), Collins (1981), and Gordon (1981, 1989). From these beginnings, this field reflected the methodological diversity of its host discipline and included leading authors and texts that drew from a range of sociological perspectives and a diversity of psychological models.[2] For the discipline as a whole, the new sociology of emotions also signified a turn to topics that resonated with the political and cultural ethos of the late 1960s and the 1970s. Sociology has always been a discipline that is peculiarly permeable to changes in the moral and political temper of the time, which in the period of the late 1960s and early 1970s resonated with antinomian themes, celebrations of social conflict, deviant subcultures, and human liberation from social "roles," from political "oppressions," and from "society" itself (Kemper 1990, 3–4). The emotions could be seen as a topic that intuitively belonged in the vicinity of these concerns, whether because the emotions represented the domain of nature or the unsocialized or because the emotions served as a data for exposing that ever-elusive authentic self—themes I will return to later.

THE CONCEPT OF CULTURE IN THE SOCIOLOGY OF EMOTIONS

But the social study of the emotions represented far more than this, however much these preoccupations about "selfhood" and "identity" weighed on our collective minds and souls. This vibrant new field of the sociology of emotions became one of the places for testing the new approaches identified with the movement called "social constructionism" and the burgeoning and influential fields known as "culture theory" and "cultural studies." Both fields have become the loci for investigations in linguistics, the humanities, and the social sciences whose common focus has been the interpretation of culture and its operations (Rabinow and Sullivan [1979] 1987; Alexander and Seidman 1990; Denzin 1992; Crane 1994; Cerulo 2002). While the early work in the sociology of emotions reflected the methodological diversity of sociology itself, more recently the sociology of emotions has taken a rather sharp "cultural turn" and has been dominated by a number of constructionist works.[3]

In fact, precisely at the same time that the sociology of emotions emerged in the early 1980s, the field of the sociology of culture was gaining ground to become one of the leading sections of the American Sociological Association, a fact that can be seen as a register of the growth of culturally based approaches to a wide range of sociological studies. This is not to say that the concept of "culture" was marginal to American sociology throughout its development. More accurately, for most of its history mainstream sociologists held "culture" as one of its key concepts while conducting much of its work without reference to its actual operations. In the influential terms of Thomas Kuhn, "normal sociology" operated without reference to culture's importance, while a number of social theorists gave it a central place within the discipline's official perspective.[4]

Then, along with a number of other disciplines, from about the period of the 1970s to the present, the study of culture shifted to become sociology's central theme. This has required a rethinking of what "culture" (the sociological concept and theory) means, a reinvention of its main features and operations, and a repositioning of a number of subfields—the sociology of science, knowledge, art, religion, and popular culture—from the margins to the center of sociological investigation.[5] Among the many things this "cultural turn" (Robertson 1992; Bonnell and Hunt 1999) signified for social science was that social phenomena do not exist in their own right, but are *produced* and *communicated*, their meanings derived in and through culture and its operations. This claim has brought the exploration and use of language theory (e.g., linguistics, semiotics) to the forefront of social-scientific inquiries. It is summarized in the "constructionist" premise that every aspect of a society is something communicated and reproduced, including the domain of the psychological, a society's notion of personhood, and the prevailing discourses through which human beings experience and articulate the meanings of feeling states. In sociological studies of American character and identity, a field that has enjoyed a rich and long history in American social psychology (Bell 1991, 167–83; Inkeles and Levinson 1969), constructionism effectively shifted this field's focus from the formative role of social institutions (social structure) in shaping the American character to studies of the cultural features of "selfhood" and "identity," reflecting the relatively new approaches offered by the fields of linguistics, anthropology, and semiotics.[6]

Central to constructionism is the claim—a claim also found in works of the American pragmatists and "interactionists" (Shalin 1986)—that the objects of social science are neither neutral nor unchanging. They are part of a meaningful universe, one that envelops both social-scientific observers and the actors they observe. This proposition led to the idea that social science is—both in its methods and in its theories of social meaning—cultural to the core (Reed and Alexander 2009). Accordingly, the very methods of studying social objects (whether persons or things) must account for their social and historical formation and reformation. This idea has been with US sociology throughout its history: it was what the early American sociologist Charles Horton Cooley had in mind when he described the institutions sociology studies as "definite and established phase[s] of the public mind, not different ... from public opinion." They are "apperceptive systems" or collective attitudes. Only by abstraction do we regard them as "things in themselves" (Cooley [1909] 1962, 313–14). Similarly, the pragmatist philosopher George Herbert Mead formulated the idea that the "things" human beings produce are "social objects"; their status—their reality—is determined in the process of interaction in particular "situations" (sociocultural contexts): an object is a part or phase of an experienced world (Mead 1934, 77–9; Dewey 1936, 67). We find in these early and influential constructionist arguments the idea that the social world is made up of "social objects," *social* because they have no existence except for the specific contexts of social relations and language within which they emerge and in which they flourish or wane (Mead 1934, 78); their meaning also exists objectively within these fields (McCall and Simmons 1966, 49–52). This constructionist emphasis has effectively engaged the social scientist in three fields of study: the *language and speech* (discourses, social idioms, public opinion) in which social phenomena—whether collective practices or entire social worlds—are generated and sustained; the *knowledges* that communicate them as real; and the *social and group relations* within which they develop and occur. This cultural and cognitive emphasis that characterized many of the leading statements of the early social thinkers of the Chicago School and the "symbolic interactionist" tradition of sociology was an emphasis not given to the dominant schools of US sociology until recently.

Sociology's newfound interest in culture and communication (knowledge, language, speech, media) has been especially important in bringing sociologists into conversation with other disciplines—literary studies, communications, cultural anthropology, studies of popular culture, and the "new cultural history" (Hunt 1989; Bonnell and Hunt 1999)—as well as for taking on subject matters that require interdisciplinary approaches like the emotions. Examining the conceptual implications of structuralism and semiotics (a project sociology shares with many of these fields of inquiry), scholars have given greater attention today to studies of the *forms of signification*, including signs, symbols, texts, images, and ideologies. These types of inquiries have ushered in changes in the ways that many sociologists today understand and conceptualize culture and its operations, as well as changes in the foundational assumptions and presuppositions of the social sciences (Sewell 1999; Eagleton 2000; Alexander 2003). Yesterday's "attitude of analysis" was causal and explanatory, and its privileged model was natural science. Today's attitude is increasingly interpretive and conversational, seeking to enlarge the universe of human discourse. This is the aim of a *semiotic concept of culture*, by which I mean one directed toward the study of the symbolic and signifying systems through which a social order is experienced and communicated.[7]

My intention in this introductory statement on the study of emotions is to demonstrate what a cultural sociology can look like—how its object can be construed and what it can study—and, at the same time, to argue for its return to current works in emotion studies, whether inside or outside of sociology proper. This argument takes up and advances some of my early statements on emotions—"Emotions Are Social Things" (1989), "The Social Construction of Emotion" (1994), and "Emotions: Senses of the Modern Self" (2002)—on the importance of culture in understanding emotions and feelings, an emphasis that seems today to have been lost in my own field of sociology, where cultural approaches are set alongside of other sociological approaches to emotions as if they are either similar or equally

valid approaches to emotion studies (Turner and Stets 2005, 23–5).
On this point I disagree: theories and methods in emotions studies do
not exist on equal or the same footing; to elaborate how culture
matters where the emotions are concerned means, inter alia, that
the object of our emotion studies changes just as its methods of
inquiry change. No other field than cultural sociology rests on this
presupposition.

In putting forward a cultural approach to the study of emotions
in these pages, I am arguing, contrary to many others, that the most
important features of our current landscape can only be understood by
taking culture seriously: our emotional lives today are our own, culturally and historically unique to our time and place in the postmodern world; emotions, as with all our experiences, are shaped by our
ideas of what a person is and can be. Emotions are inextricably linked
to what we call identity; emotions have become part of "being
emotional" and "acting emotional," meaningful phrases in our
current vocabulary. And these are not phrases familiar to the everyday
vocabulary of either my mother or my grandmothers.

My argument, in a nutshell, is that emotions are—as objects of
our sciences—inescapably and without remainder cultural objects,
however much we know and feel them "as our own" (or as someone
else's). Put differently, emotions are social things because they belong
to the entire domain of culture and human meaning. But let me now
get on with the business of advancing this argument.

Arguably, the most significant feature of this new cultural
(semiotic) disposition for the social sciences has been its root metaphor of *construction*: the idea that the realities we study are socially
produced. If emotions, for example, are "social constructs," then their
construction and constructors can be looked into (Hacking 1999;
Gergen 2009; Lincoln and Guba 2013). Culture, in all its complex
and many-layered facets, is something (actually, many things) explicit
or recorded (Crane 1994, 2–4); that is, culture exists in *things* such as
print journalism, electronic media, and an entire range of artifacts
from art to food, from clothing to scientific data. This has been one

of the culturists' most consequential claims: namely, that culture, in all of its forms—its aesthetic tendencies and its material artifacts, its bodily dispositions, its sacred and profane iconography, its laws, and its sciences—are things produced or constructed. Here I am alluding to Berger and Luckmann's (1966) influential treatise in the sociology of knowledge, *The Social Construction of Reality*. Since its publication almost five decades ago, the idea of a "constructed reality" (or realities) has summarized and advanced further a number of contemporary themes in social science. Among these themes, undoubtedly its most consequential for sociology, is *the problem of meaning and the use of philosophical, literary, and historical approaches to the study of the social construction of meaning* (McCarthy 1996, 20–2).

As I argue here, interest in the problem of meaning, an interest that effectively redefined the fundamental premises on which most of sociology has been built, is linked to a methodological framework that is neither causal nor explanatory but one that is semiotic. Accordingly, a society or social order (and, indeed, a self, an identity, and what we refer to as an emotional life) is viewed as something communicated and reproduced through a people's collective practices, particularly their symbolic and signifying systems. These signifying systems and practices are what make up a culture and its structure of meaning. Culture, then, is not something derived from "society" or "social structure," as earlier sociologists claimed. Rather, culture—in the form of a society's signifying systems—is the means through which a social order is established and maintained. In the words of Raymond Williams (1981, 12–13), an early and influential proponent of this position:

> "Cultural practice" and "cultural production" ... are not simply derived from an otherwise constituted social order but are themselves major elements in its constitution ... It sees culture as the *signifying system* through which necessarily (though among other means) a social order is communicated, reproduced, experienced and explored.

With this twofold interest, *first*, in the semiotics of culture and, *second*, in its production, the field of cultural studies has examined the observable properties of knowledges and symbols in texts, modes of communication, and forms of speech, each of these linked to specific institutional frameworks (Peterson 1976, 1994). Culture is studied in the many and diverse symbolic products of particular institutions and groups, such as those of religious practitioners, journalists, psychoanalysts, social workers, scientists, academics, and lawyers. So whatever else we do through our sciences and our professions (and, surely, a "whatever else" of profound consequences), cultural studies examines how what is produced through these knowledges *is* culture: how cultural practices, artifacts, and texts are hammered together, whether elaborate religious cosmologies, cuisines, forms of bodily decorum, organized games and sports, but also our psychologies and anthropologies; *all of these phenomena communicate and signify cultural meanings and messages.* For every aspect of social life can serve as a cultural form providing messages and meanings: all aspects of human life serve as *modes of signification* that dispense collective images and ideas. This is no less true of our everyday or unofficial cultural forms—those of the popular and the mass—as of our official ones—like religion, science, literature, and law (McCarthy 1996, 25–6).

EMOTIONS AS SOCIAL CONSTRUCTS

In the study of the emotions, constructionism's emphasis is on the cognitive and cultural features of emotion, an emphasis it shares with many cognitive psychologists working in emotion studies (see Reddy 2001, ch. 1) and with those identified with early works in the social constructionist movement in psychology (Gergen 1985; Gergen and Davis 1985; Averill 1980, 1986) and its early and influential statements on the philosophy and psychology of emotions (Harré 1986), as well as with a number of early emotion studies in cultural anthropology (Lutz 1988; Shweder and LeVine 1984) and philosophy (de Sousa 1987; Rorty 1980; Solomon 1976, 1984) of the same period.[8]

Proponents of this approach have argued that emotions cannot divorced from the sociocultural meanings in which they are experienced and expressed. That is, while we can *analytically* distinguish emotions from bodily and cognitive functions and processes, emotions are best grasped as objects of investigation within the domain of cultural forms and meanings. Furthermore, constructionists argue that the linkages of affect and cultural form are vital for both conceptualizing emotions and for studying their operations. It is in this sense that emotions cannot be divorced from cultural phenomena: from "vocabularies of emotion" (H. Geertz, 1959) or the rules governing expression and feeling, from the idioms (both theoretical and pretheoretical) within which they are experienced and expressed (and the degrees of refinement each of these take), and from the cultural patterns and interactional processes within which they emerge and are sustained (Gordon 1990). In these different senses, emotions are described as cognitive and evaluative phenomena, for they are articulated to self and others—discursively and gesturally— (Perinbanayagam 1989, 1991, 2011). That is, emotions communicate and signal things about self and society in the larger sense of a shared culture or in the immediate, situational sense of, say, Erving Goffman's "interaction order" (1983, 1967, 1–3), the domain of face-to-face interactions.

In fact, it was Goffman who advanced the argument that emotions are important signs or signifiers of the self and its *character* (1967, 149–270): character is up for grabs or at risk because it emerges out of social situations and refers "to attributes that can be generated and destroyed during fateful moments" (1967, 238). In fact, many of the social situations we enter in everyday life demand that we be ready for the situations that arise, that successful management of these roles and situations requires knowing what will occur, what is at stake, and whether or not one's character will be "acquired or lost" (1967, 237–9). In chapter 2 we will return to some of Goffman's accounts of the social self that bear most directly on his dramaturgical approach to identity.

Steven Gordon (1981, 562; cf. 1989), one of the first to system-atize a sociology of emotions, identified what he termed the "socially emergent properties of emotions that transcend psychological and/or physiological explanation." Emotions, he argued, combine features of body, gesture, and cultural meaning. The sociology-of-emotions project involves the study of how emotions are differentiated, socia-lized, and managed. Gordon's early thinking on this matter is repre-sentative of a number of current constructionist approaches, viewing emotions as inextricably social or cultural, precisely because they are emergent properties of social relations and sociocultural processes. In fact, among later sociologists of emotions, this emphasis on the cultural aspects of emotions has been sustained among some of the field's leading spokesmen.[9]

These arguments rest upon a distinctly *cultural set of presuppo-sitions*. One of these emphasizes the "autonomy" of culture from social structure, an argument made, inter alia, in early statements by Jeffrey Alexander (1990) and William Sewell (1999): cultural forms cannot be read from (or reduced to) social behavior or social organiza-tion. They are patterns in their own right; they cannot be explained deductively by reference to a set of factors that are outside of culture. Accordingly, emotions do not exist as something apart from the cul-tural forms that describe them. For there are no "natural objects" of inquiry in the human sciences (Hunt 1989, 7; cf. Klein 2006; Gallant 2012). In the terms of social pragmatism, emotions are *social objects* whose meanings exist within a system of relations. Emotions or entire complexes of emotions "unfold in a world already symbolized" and are constructed as *what they* are "by the concept[s]" we have of them.[10] According to another formulation, emotions operate as "discursive objects"; they emerge within a discourse, an organization of written and spoken forms, areas of language-use identified by parti-cular historical groups and institutions: the discourses of professions, such as psychology and medicine; or academic and theoretical discourses, such as philosophy and literary studies; or metatheoretical discourses, such as liberal humanism, which shares underlying assumptions from modern utilitarianism, rationalism, and empiricism. The "truths" about emotions, the self, and so forth are contained within the operations of these discourses and are, in turn, experienced on the pretheoretical level by the subjects who live them as truths. In this way, language and discourse are both the foundation and the instruments of the social construction of subjective and objective reality, as Peter Berger (1970, 376) argued in his early and influential statement on the "social construction of identity."

Contemporary theories of culture also set clear limits to inquiries into causes and into universal foundations, but they also undermine phenomenological and psychological views of "subjectivity," since subjectivity itself (personal experiences, perceptions, judgments, etc.) is always given form and voice through social categories and discourses. Language categories and cultural meanings are no longer viewed "subjectively." For they share "a kind of objectivity which is not the objectivity of things, [they share] a kind of idea which is not the idea of a subjective mind" (Harland 1987, 68; cf. Bourdieu's [1979] 1984 critique of subjectivity in *Distinction*).

Following these arguments, it is culture theory that provides the framework and the presuppositions for examining how our own "languages" of selfhood and our own Western proclivity to divide up our worlds (and ourselves) into "subjects" and "objects" (or "subjective" and "objective") imply a distinct idiom of emotion, one, incidentally, that is enshrined in our philosophies, psychologies, and social-scientific categories. Accordingly, the cultural approach to emotions that I argue here is *not* best characterized as an approach that examines the cultural factors (language, beliefs, values, etc.) that shape people's (otherwise unshaped) emotional experiences. Rather, in keeping with the arguments of cultural studies, my own cultural argument about the emotions is directed toward understanding precisely how discourse, image, and sign situate people relative to their own experiences and actions: the emotions they feel, how they express them, what these feelings mean to them. A cultural approach views the social self as an experiencing self who is simultaneously a "person with feelings" and a reader of emotional signs, one's own and those of others. And it is culture that provides the system of meanings, the "structure" within which emotions and feelings, moods and dispositions, gestures and grimaces can be read and understood *as* something: an argument made by Alexander (1990) and elaborated throughout his more recent works (Alexander 2010; Alexander, Jacobs, and Smith 2012).

This approach examines how other and important features of emotional experience—a society's or group's category of the person, its ideas about emotions themselves (if such exist at all), its notions about the meaning and intensity of feelings, its ideas about speaking about one's feelings to others (in private and in public, if we are describing our own social world)—frame emotional experiences themselves and the responses that people have to their own and others' emotions. In these ways, culture (to speak holistically about something both diverse and disparate) is not something added to the emotions. Emotions—what they mean, how they are experienced—are cultural from the start. For they emerge within particular cultural contexts which render them as what they really are, that is, how they are collectively thought and known to be and how they are supposed to be felt and expressed. To borrow and reapply what Foucault argued about sexual behaviors (O'Higgins and Foucault 1984, 10–11): *Feelings and emotions are more than we think they are. They are the consciousness we have of what we feel, what we make of these feelings, and the values we attach to these feelings.*

To further characterize emotion studies within this framework, the emotions, as with all social-psychological phenomena, are examined in and through the study of everyday notions about emotions and the self and through the entire range of discourses (religious, scientific, therapeutic, etc.) that define and frame people's experiences and sentiments. This approach, taken up by researchers in sociology, anthropology, and history, has given greater emphasis to studies of "emotional cultures," "emotionology" (popular standards and practices about emotions and to folk psychology), and "ethnopsychology" (the ideas and understandings that ordinary people draw from to understand their feelings and emotions)—terms identified with pioneering works in this field. This cultural emphasis has effectively displaced the focus from the study of emotions *themselves* to the discursive operations that constitute our "emotional lives," the cultural practices and settings in which emotions are known, controlled, cultivated, and worked on. This approach, incorporating a number of distinct but interrelated sets of concerns, examines, for example, the social standards used in the cultivation, expression, and control of human feelings and emotions and, most importantly, examines the sources of various cultures of emotion in religion, science, medical and therapeutic practice and discourse, as well as in popular and folk (traditional) practices. Furthermore, emotions are the products of *social knowledges* and are strategically linked to the authorities that disseminate knowledges—such as parent, priest, teacher, or therapist. These authorities serve as *educators of the emotions*, teaching people what the emotions mean, how they are to be expressed and managed, and what they signify.

In contrast to early debates in the sociology of emotions concerning *how much culture matters* (see Thoits 1989, 319), today's inquiries ask, "*How* does culture matter where the emotions are concerned?" What are the particular cultural and ideological contexts in which the emotions are identified and constituted? What are the authoritative institutions and cultures within which emotions and the self are experienced as what they are and what they mean? How do the contours of selfhood today (its preoccupation with autonomy and authenticity, its celebration of freedom and release from constraints, its pursuit of self-esteem and personal empowerment) help us to understand why feelings and emotions today have become not only a vital aspect of what we call authentic personhood but powerful cultural objects as well?

Arguments for a *history of emotions* follow logically upon a constructionist approach to the emotions. For it is in and through (historically particular) cultural systems that emotions have come into being *as something*, that is, as objects of experiences that *mean* something, and as a differentiated system of signs with which the self engages. A history of emotions is particularly suited to address questions of how precisely and in what ways *cultures of sentiment and emotion* (standards, ideas, precepts concerning how to feel, what to feel, and what feelings mean) and *emotional experiences* themselves actually change and what these changes signify.

Peter Stearns summarized the relationship of constructionism and the study of history of emotions this way: "History and historical sociology, along with cultural comparisons, provide the clearest empirical basis for constructionist approaches to emotion" (P. Stearns 1994, 308). This is because culture not only helps us to clarify what emotion is and how it actually operates relative to cultural processes, culture matters "a great deal in directing emotional responses and evaluations according to changing social needs." Changes in feelings and emotions also occur, because the emotions are the products of collective acts of interpretation; this is also a way of understanding the social self. To know how and what to feel, to be conscious of emotional experiences is, to cite Walker Percy (1958), to be "conscious of something being something." Emotions and feelings come into being *as something*, that is, as social or cultural objects of our experiences that *mean* something and as a differentiated system of signs with which persons engage. This returns us to the *system of culture* in which any object—an emotion, a person, an event—is known and interpreted *as something*. The emotions, for example, have a range of historical meanings closely associated with aspirations concerning self-control, with religious salvation or redemption, with self-integration or wholeness, with one's moral goodness or sinfulness, and with the meanings a person gives to her ability to control what she feels and how she feels it.

Finally, another emphasis of the cultural model—one that my own study draws from—is the idea that culture, rather than operating holistically, is best understood through the notion of "practice," "cultural practice," or "performance." This approach—formulated first in works by Pierre Bourdieu ([1972]1977), Stuart Hall (1980), and William Sewell (1999)—locates culture in *acts* or *practices* dispersed throughout the social order, rather than viewing culture as in consciousness or in nonmaterial social facts as traditionally conceived. The concept "cultural practice" renders culture as observable: culture is material, culture is *done*, as much as thought and felt. Accordingly, culture is diverse, many layered, and multi-coded, accessible for study in many forms and sites: in practitioners' settings, in photos and films, in sports arenas, in romance novels, in forms of talk, and in our forms of memorializing, just as it is enshrined in our sciences and our literary texts. This contemporary (poststructuralist) idea of culture—coming as it does in the footsteps of Claude Lévi-Strauss, Louis Althusser, and Roland Barthes—uses language as its theoretical and empirical model, the system and process for the study of how representation occurs. Stuart Hall (1980, 30) explains the significance of this linguistic model for the social sciences:

> Language, which is the medium for the production of meaning, is both an ordered or "structured" system and a means of "expression." It could be rigorously and systematically studied—but not within the framework of a simple set of determinacies. Rather, it had to be analyzed as a structure of variant possibilities, the arrangement of elements in a signifying chain, as a "practice" not expressing the world (that is, reflecting it in words) but articulating it, articulated upon it. Lévi-Strauss used this model to decipher the languages (myths, culinary practices and so on) of so-called "primitive" societies. Barthes offered a more informal "semiotics," studying the systems of signs and representations in an array of languages, codes and everyday practices in contemporary societies. Both brought the term "culture" down from its abstract heights to the level of the "anthropological," the everyday.

STUDYING EMOTIONS AS CULTURAL PRACTICES

Several leading studies by sociologists and psychologists of the emotions address the general question of *how and why the emotions are important in today's world* (Barbalet 1998; Illouz 1997, 2007, 2008; Lupton 1998; McCarthy 2002; S. Williams 2001; Oatley 2004, ch. 8). Each of these authors describes, in different ways and terms, the growing popular and scientific interest in emotions along with a sense of the *displacement* of emotion and feeling in today's world through processes of self-control and emotion management. By "displacement" I mean that controlling and managing our emotions, so much a part of modern and postmodern selfhood, leave us feeling as if we have not really felt deeply at all. In this context, Barbalet has observed, "It is not surprising . . . that much of the current sociology of emotions is focused on the problems of emotion management" (1998, 176), referring to the idea of "managing" our emotions first identified by Hochschild (1983). It might even be said that one of the core problems—social as well as personal—today is "control" of ourselves and, especially, our emotions; this is the centerpiece of Peter Stearns's 1999 study, the struggle for self-control in a world where pleasure and fun compete with our deeply felt need to reign ourselves in. Or, according to Daniel Bell's (1996) now-classic portrait of the cultural contradictions of late capitalism, we are driven by the logic of our culture to pursue ourselves, while in the domain of the workplace self-restraints still operate.

With some exceptions, sociologists were silent on the topic of emotions until relatively recently when it appeared across a wide range of specializations: in popular culture, studies of television talk shows (Lowney 1999; Illouz 2003a, 2003b); in studies of intense emotions involved in social movements (Goodwin, Jasper, and Polletta 2001); in mass media where entertainment and celebrity rule and transform news and politics (Gabler 1998; Kellner 1995, 2003a, 2003b); in sports and leisure where emotions are aroused (Dunning 1999; Hanin 1999); and in studies of emotions in everyday life (Katz

1999; Swidler 2001; Oatley and Duncan 1994). Emotions are seen as integral to our leisure, fun, and mass-produced utopias (Illouz 1997). "Capitalist culture" and its consumer culture have become, arguably since the mid-twentieth century, a powerful carrier of a culture of hedonism, pleasure, and release (Bell 1996; Illouz 1997, 2007, 2008; Ritzer 2004). These are some of the themes of contemporary socio-logical studies of emotions in postmodernity.

In several important respects, these studies have begun to capture, descriptively, today's emotional culture and how it has become a culture distinguished by so many "emotional pursuits" (in leisure, sports, consumption, etc.). It can even be said that we live today in a world of emotions, a world where psychology (its perspec-tives and its vocabulary) has become part of everyday life and speech and of the stories we tell about ourselves (Plummer 1995; Gregoire 2014): on radio and television talk shows; in the offices of practitioners from whom we seek advice about our "emotional lives"; in the exchanges we have with friends and intimates about what we feel, how deeply we feel, and what these feelings mean. Despite the vastly different emotional forms and sites of these examples, they share in common certain features of postmodern identity: *we are in important ways constituted by our emotions and feelings.* Self-expression, particularly the expression of our feelings and emotions, is an expres-sion of our most real selves. Emotions and feelings—"getting emotions out" and "emotional pursuits"—are vital aspects of today's cultural practices as well as of each person's "emotional habitus" (Kane 1997, 2001).

Emotional Lives examines the emotions today as cultural prac-tices and what these practices mean within the context of social life in the postmodern world. What particularly interests me is how certain features of public life have become marked by public displays of emotionality in recent decades—from about the 1970s to today—when others were identifying the emergence of certain distinguishing features of postmodernity (sometimes called late capitalism, postin-dustrial society, late modernity, high modernity): globalization; its information technologies; its service- and knowledge-based econo-mies; its cultures of consumption, leisure, and pleasure; its environ-ment of signs and images; and so forth. These are the contexts, as I will argue, in which our emotional lives have assumed their contemporary meaning.

In public life we witness collective displays of emotions that point to a new or changed *culture of emotions* today: the rise of spectator sports and their mass consumption by fans (Guttman 2004); the emotionally intense displays associated with rock and rap concerts (Woody 2012); the emotions provoked, displayed, and manipulated during political campaigns and conventions; the rise of new forms of public monuments and memorials ("shrines to senti-ment"); and the building of new museums to mark and to remember assassinations, atrocities, and human disasters. These very public cultural forms and sites are my principal focus; they are visible to all of us but neither studied nor interpreted as important emotional forms in their own right. In fact, I am impressed by their absence in socio-logical and historical studies of today's emotional cultures.

However, I examine these against a background—one to which I will regularly return—of everyday life that is also marked by an environment of emotional images and messages. The television ads we watch and the radio talk shows we listen to provide a constant parade of people, images, voices, and sounds designed to offer us pleasure and other forms of stimulation (or its promise) while enter-taining us. And let's not forget the reality TV shows that offer us alternative lives. The new forms and sites of consuming goods and fun, called "landscapes of consumption" (Ritzer 2004), offer us plea-sures and delights while shopping at immense malls, gambling at the new casino parks, vacationing at theme parks, and eating at theme restaurants. This emotional environment (of promises and delights) is also a one where psychology has become a mass idiom and where feelings are the topic of our endless chatter, as well as one of the principal topics for which we seek advice about our "emotional lives" from those we "consult" in living color (Dr. Ruth or Dr. Phil on TV; online advice from Carolyn Hax or Always Marsha). It is online and on TV that we are told ("tele-advised") by Oprah—in her new media venues—about how to improve our lives (Illouz 2003; McGee 2005). In everyday life, emotions, as we say today, are "out there," as things we know about, matters that draw our efforts and our attention, things of such value that an entire science is given over to their investigation (psychology), and a virtual army of practitioners exists solely for their skillful and humane application. This is how most of us "know" about emotions. It is a media-generated and media-driven knowledge that forms the backdrop for our more public emotional displays.

The mass media have become an important dimension of everyday life that is integral to many of the emotional pursuits I study (Doveling, von Scheve, and Konijn, 2011); everyday life is played out against what Todd Gitlin (2002, 14) has effectively portrayed as a "shimmering" background: "images and sounds, emanating from television, videotapes, videodisks, video games" but also portable electronics like car radios and CD players, iPods, and cell phones that allow us to be plugged in almost continuously to an environment of images, messages, voices, and sounds to stimulate and entertain us. Since my study began, I have come to see the mass media as elements in the development of many of these new and public displays of emotion. In fact, some of these collective behaviors have emerged out of new forms of media-based social identities where "participants" and "audiences" are inextricably part of the practice or event. Some examples:

In the pursuit of "extreme games" in leisure and competitive sports, for example, websites like Everestnews.com keep audiences and journalists informed about the latest news on current climbs and climbers; leading climbers author bestselling books and become media personalities, such as Jon Krakauer, author of *Into Thin Air*. When in 1999 Tori Murden became the first woman rower to cross an ocean—the Atlantic Ocean on the *American Pearl*—she was one of the first athletes who competed while posting messages on her website as her "onlookers" sent messages of emotional support. Diana Nyad's 2013 swim from Havana to Key West is recorded on YouTube; her 110-mile swim lit up Facebook and Twitter with postings and congratulations.

Or, take the collective and highly emotional responses of individuals and groups to the heroics of firefighters—such as when six firefighters in Worcester, Massachusetts (December 6, 1999), gave up their lives while searching a burning building for homeless people. This event and the public displays that followed it, which were made possible by the Internet and email—President Clinton and other dignitaries joined thirty thousand firefighters from around the world in a three-mile funeral procession—enabled firefighters worldwide to form "communities," to "gather" online, to assemble, to march, and to be viewed (and to view themselves) if not in living color then in cyberspace.

There are many examples of the firefighter heroes and the media dramas and the iconography of these heroes, especially, the mediatized police and firefighter funeral processions that follow many of today's disasters. Edward Linenthal, for example, provided extensive historical treatment in his study of the Oklahoma City National Memorial's iconography of the firefighter hero (Linenthal 2001). Other more recent commemorations of these heroes come to mind like the March 2014 fire on Beacon Street in Boston after which ten thousand firefighters from across the United States and some from as far away as Australia stood at attention as a fire truck carried the remains of Lt. Edward Walsh, a forty-three-year-old fireman who died in the fire that trapped him and fellow fireman Michael Kennedy.

Mass media—photos, films, televised and online ceremonies—are vital to the formation of these cultural heroes, these "risk-takers," and the powerful collective emotions they evoke; emotional media dramas express and articulate the meaning of these current-day heroes to the public and to participants. Take the other recent example: the August 2013 Rim Fire of 150,000 acres near Yosemite National Park, California, generated multiple photo postings tagged "2013

Wildfire." But perhaps the gravest images and postings to honor these heroes followed upon the deaths of the nineteen firefighters only months before, when members of the Prescott Fire Department's Granite Mountain Hotshots were killed (June 30, 2013) while fighting the Yarnell Hill fire, northwest of Phoenix. The amount of news coverage and the number of photos and videos following this event were massive, as were the postings of online memorials "honoring the dead." (See state websites like that of the California Firefighters Association.)

Consider the new emotional sites—both popular and assembled by public and state institutions—to memorialize and to remember deaths, wars, human disasters. Sometimes it is to commemorate the death of a celebrity or statesman (Princess Diana of Wales serves as the prototype) by masses of mourners and mass audiences. Sometimes—with air crashes—commemorations take place to mark the site where unknown victims fell; in other cases, to mark the deaths in 1999 of known victims, the Columbine High School students. Both actual sites and virtual sites have become the location for displays, sites for memorializing, for "hanging our feelings" (Gross 1999: 3), and for the gatherings in cyberspace of those who want to participate in these memorial events as they occur.

The recent and widely covered and felt 2012 shooting deaths of twenty schoolchildren and six adult staff members at the Sandy Hook Elementary School in December 2012 is remarkable in so many ways, including the efforts of town residents to resist and control mass media coverage of this event on its anniversary dates, a resistance that confirms a widespread sense today of the power of mass media over our lives (and deaths).

Today's forms of pleasure and play have also taken an emotional turn of some intensity: take the mania of fans inside and outside stadiums, like the displays before and following the World Series victories of the Boston Red Sox, first in 2004, then in 2007 and in 2013; or, the now-legendary 1998 home run race of Mark McGuire and

Sammy Sosa to beat Roger Maris's record. The expression and display of intense emotions figured in the excitement of fans, but also, and especially, they found expression with McGuire and Sosa themselves, whose displays of strong feelings on the field, recorded simultaneously on gigantic stadium digital screens, were striking and unprecedented, particularly when seen against the personal reserve of earlier baseball heroes of similar accomplishment. The 1961 films of Roger Maris—his demeanor and reserve—replayed during the 1998 competition, provided dramatic studies in the contrast of emotional cultures then and now, of celebrity athletes and their fans. (Billy Crystal's acclaimed film "61*" about this home run race in 1961 premiered in 2001; it was re-released on Blu-ray DVD in 2011.)

Cultural practices like these can be used as resources for identifying today's emotional cultures. Emotional cultures are embedded, as it were, in these practices, as are moral self-understandings, notions of self and identity: that is, who I *really* am (whatever that "really" refers to), *how* the self is construed, *what* it believes itself to be, *how* it is connected (or not connected) to other selves, whether or not it believes in its own individuality. All of these aspects of identity as well as others are closely related to what I mean here by "emotional cultures."

When examined together cultural practices like these begin to capture, descriptively, today's particular "structure of feeling" (R. Williams 1961, 48) and how it has become a culture distinguished by so many emotional pursuits (in leisure, consumption, sports, politics, human relations). Finally, I am proposing here not only a significant shift in emotional cultures in the last half century (about the mid-twentieth century to today) but also changes in the notions of the person or the social self of the same period and an accompanying change in emotionality—more reflexive (and modeled on both media messages and images) as well as fueled by the culture of consumerism that drives Daniel Bell's "post-industrial society" and its contradictions of rationality and emotionality built into the domains of today's culture, polity, and economy (Bell 1996).

Emotional Lives includes an examination of how public emotional displays point to certain changes taking place in collective notions of private life and the public life: how media culture generates new forms of social and personal relationships and deep attachments to celebrity hosts and stars; how, for example, museums and memorials (chapter 3), once sites marked by aesthetic and personal reserve and formality, have become places where publics expect to experience and to relive ("personally") events not only of the historical past but of contemporary disasters, tragedies, and victimhood. Consider, for example, the Holocaust museums; the JFK museum in Dallas; the Oklahoma City memorial; and Sandy Hook Elementary School in Newtown, Connecticut, the town itself and the now-demolished school, sites of the 2012 killings of twenty schoolchildren and six adult workers at the school. Despite the vastly different emotional forms and sites of these examples, they share in common certain features of postmodern culture and its particular structure of feeling. Of course, it is only through such an approach as the one I propose here— a cultural and collective approach to emotions—that these new and very public forms of emotional drama and display can be studied, like the emotions of sports fans at Super Bowls or of those crowds of mourners for Princess Diana, or those groups of joyful Catholics in the Piazza San Pietro, awaiting news of the election of Pope Francis in 2013.

However, my attempt here is to do more than point to important cultural practices that are replete with emotional content—happiness, joy, pleasure, anger, feelings of pleasure and desire, or of aggression and violence. Nor am I content to describe the cultural (mass media) and structural (economic and institutional) sources of these changes in the emotional cultures of contemporary societies. Rather, I am arguing here that these cultural practices, these very public activities, share something in common, that they represent something new on the cultural terrain, and that they draw from and reproduce in our contemporary world a notion of the person (the "individual") that, while continuous with features of the "modern individual," represent something that departs from its earlier manifestations.

I describe this new concept of the person as one modeled on and responsive to today's media culture. This concept of the "person"—an "ideal type" (in Max Weber's sense of the term)—is a way of describing certain features of the self (and the self-concept) of our contemporary American culture and civilization; it is antinomian—anti-institutional—in disposition, just as its preferred mode of action is self-seeking and impulsive. It seeks to express and to discover itself in the "environments"—media images and dramas (TV programs, movies)—it consumes, just as it has become skilled in the consumption of the various pursuits and pleasures of our culture. As I will argue here, collective acts like these operate as signs of a new phase of modern subjectivity, a new way of thinking about ourselves and our society, a "social imaginary." This new way of construing self and society—perhaps only decades old—seeks to overcome or to eclipse the distance and separation between the self or subject and the object viewed, to overcome the separation of the viewer and the object experienced. Postmodernity and its media culture disrupt the order of things, the primacy of outside reality as *there* and ourselves as distanced onlookers. It rearranges space (foreground and background) and beckons spectators to engage as participants in emotional dramas of affirmation and discovery

A final word on the book's central argument *that our lives today are distinguished by a distinctive and intense emotionality and a number of culturally significant emotional pursuits*. This argument appears to contradict the claims of a number of contemporary studies, such as Arlie Hochschild's (1983) influential account of the "commercialization of human feeling" and Peter Stearns's (1994) argument that since mid-century we have been undergoing an important sea change, the emergence of a distinctly American emotional style, "cool."

The arguments I present here are, in many ways, compatible with these authors' claims. In fact, if there is any merit to the argument that in many features of American life today we witness an unprecedented demonstration of emotionality—a change in the way we readily display and pursue our pleasures and enjoyments, our frenzies of fun and feeling—it will be found in the ways I interpret this argument in conversations with the works of others who have ventured into this uncharted territory of postmodern emotionality.

Arlie Hochschild's (1983) now-classic portrait of service workers, women employees like flight attendants, shows us how job-based "emotion work" imposes controls on workers' spontaneous feelings and how such emotion work extracts its costs well beyond the workplace. For it affects our capacity to respond to our feelings and even our capacity to feel at all. This portrait has important implications for the workplace but also for an entire society where managing our emotions and being "emotionally intelligent" (Goleman 1995) has become a prerequisite for daily living. As Hochschild observes, we "have become adept at recognizing and discounting commercialized feeling . . . . [and] *we 'place an unprecedented value on "spontaneous" natural feeling'* (1983, 189–90, emphasis added).

It is this last point that is the focus of my own work—today's *culture of emotions and the self*: how we have come to place a special value on our feelings and on *knowing our feelings*; how the self in its postmodern manifestations has come to be commonly understood as the *feeling* or *emotional self*; how we have become, in Irving Howe's (1967, p. 31) memorable phrase, persons "entranced with depths," our own; how, in a relatively short span of time, a new social type was born, one who claimed to have and to live an "emotional life."

Peter Stearns's (1994) account of us as "cool" characters is an important contribution to today's emotional culture, as is his related study of our active pursuits of self-control (1999). He has approached the problem of today's emotional culture and its changes from a very different direction than my own. His "behavioral history" takes us back to profound changes in our ideas and feelings about emotions in the decades from the 1920s to the 1960s and beyond. His work has been important to my own thinking about changing emotional cultures in the twentieth century. We differ principally in our focus on the developing features of postmodern life today and the very public displays of intense emotionality that we engage in as audiences and actors. (See chapter 2 below.) We are, indeed, cool characters (or we try to be), as Stearns shows us, but this cool, unflappable self competes with our yearning for *real emotions* and for a self that *really feels deeply,* to use some contemporary phrases. Or so my own argument goes.

I am also arguing against those who view the postmodern self as principally fragmented and decentered, with a kind of emotional flatness or depthlessness (e.g., Allan 1997; Wrathall and Malpas 2000, section I; Meštrović 1997; cf. Taylor 1989, 498–502), a perspective providing what I regard as a limited portrait and interpretation of our emotional experiences today. Regardless of how or whether many of us feel this emotional shallowness or emptiness at all, there are signs in our public lives that we have not given up on the pursuit of "true emotions and feelings" and of "authenticity" (Vannini and Williams 2009; McCarthy 2009). And we seek emotions in the many places where we are invited to act out our feelings as actors do, on the many stages provided by our mediatized world: the malls we walk through to the rhythm of music and the staginess of designed and mirrored runways; the concerts and plays we attend; parks and city High Lines where we parade with others in public spaces as participants in a nature-watch of our very own; the sports arenas where we experience what it is to be a true fan; the churches where we discover our faith, where we sing hymns and weep with others. Even digital sites have become our stages, like the Facebook pages and photos we arrange and rearrange *who we are* for digital audiences—ourselves, our friends, and other imagined onlookers. Today's mediatized world has allowed us to perform our feelings like actors do, to enter life itself and to discover its real dramas and to claim them as our own.

2 Emotions and Modern Identity

"Subjectivity becomes the typical condition of the modernist outlook ...
Modernism declares itself as an inflation of the self, a transcendental
and orgiastic aggrandizement of matter and event in behalf of personal
vitality."

Irving Howe (1967)

"Now and then it is possible to observe the moral life in a process of
revising itself ... perhaps by inventing and adding to itself a new element,
some mode of conduct or of feeling which hitherto it had not regarded
as essential to virtue."

Lionel Trilling (1971)

"The self has a history and a social history and that of the contemporary
emotivist self is only intelligible as the end product of a long and
complex set of developments."

Alasdair MacIntyre (1983, 31)

PRELIMINARIES

What are emotions today? As stated above (chapter 1), this question
presupposes that emotions are part of culture and social life itself, that
emotions change together with our changing worlds and technologies,
our changing experiences, and our changing identities. A brief examination from modernity's early to its contemporary history will help
us to see how, relative to our forebears, we experience our emotions
today and what our emotions mean to us.

From this perspective, it becomes apparent that the emotions
have taken on specific meanings throughout modernity's history,
that the emotions today have become special objects of attention
and elaboration for postmodern selves or "subjects," and that the
emotions are integral to postmodern identity, to the pursuit of
what we call "authenticity" or how I perceive my "real self."
What I hope to capture is what the emotions are culturally, that

is, according to our everyday sense of things, how the emotions operate as vehicles of knowledge of the world, as so many channels transmitting to our minds and consciousness both the (external) realm of reality and the realm of our personhood, what we call our *inner lives*. The emotions, I will argue, represent a new direction, a new movement, and a new location of knowledge for modern subjects—an inwardness, a new interior domain where the emotions are (thought to be) housed. Accordingly, the emotions, *as we experience them*, emanate from deep within the self, as signifiers of our inner depths and spaces, "their sublime origin" (Reddy 2001, 316; Taylor 1989, ch. 11). Emotional meanings and messages are embedded in our very public images and discourses about the good life and its pursuit, about pleasure and happiness, about having fun, about how "emotional" we should or should not act and feel around others, and with others.

A few examples drawn from different sources and subject matters will highlight some of these changes in emotions and identity throughout the modern era.

In the early modern period (sixteenth through seventeenth centuries), new rules, standards, and sensitivities about "civility" (a new word) and etiquette were elaborated (Elias [1939] 2000). These were accompanied by a self-consciousness about the process of self-monitoring and personal conduct, in particular, the comportment of one's body, alone and with others. Centered first on life in the court of the prince and the instruction of courtiers, these "new rules," and their accompanying feelings about pride, shame, and disgust, spread to other sectors of society as the class structure broadened, making, for example, Erasmus's "etiquette" for boys a sixteenth-century best seller (see also Appendix B below). Stephen Greenblatt's (1980) work on sixteenth-century self-fashioning in Renaissance England takes up themes that are remarkable in the ways they parallel and complement those of Elias on changing elements of power in early modern societies and the ways these are manifest in changing standards of behavior and feelings surrounding one's body and one's identity.

The claims of Elias on emotional change have recently been argued in a work of French literary history (DeJean 1997) where the then-new language of *sensibilité* (a greater and more intense emotionality) is used to describe changing emotional states in the novels of popular writers of the 1690s. In this time of the battle of the books, the Moderns, referring to one of the camps in this battle, worked to define literature itself by its ability to effectively portray human inner emotional struggles. DeJean's remarkable claim about the cultural significance of a French novelist, Madeleine de Scudéry, is that this author not only provided a new modern "vocabulary of upheaval" but, more than this, identified a new *emotional semantic*, a shift in the meanings of emotions themselves (DeJean 1997, 83–7; cf. Johnson-Laird and Oatley 1989). Regardless of what we make of this particular literary and historical interpretation, there is ample evidence (in lexica and encyclopedias of the eighteenth century) that the Age of Enlightenment saw the beginnings of new and important and widespread appreciations of the emotions (Frevert, 2014, 12–24).

In works on late eighteenth-century French philosophy (Taylor 1989; Reddy 2001), the rise of a new sentimentalism enters into conflict with the century's emphasis on freedom through the application of reason. Rousseau is an important source of the idea that nature is an inner voice or impulse (Taylor 1989, 368–9); emotions are extolled as both natural and, in unfettered forms, operate as signs of goodness: the happiest people are the simple people, who conduct their affairs sitting together under an oak, as in one of Rousseau's famous accounts of the natural and emotional simplicity of the uncultivated life (1968, book 4, ch. 1). In *Émile*, we read, "Everything is good as it leaves the hands of the Author of things; everything degenerates in the hands of man" (Rousseau 1970, book I).

In nineteenth-century England and America one can trace the development of a "sentimentality" expressed in a Victorian reserve in matters of feelings—a reserve that struggled with the widely accepted view of the "vitality of feelings" (Gay 1984, 455). The Victorians were an ambivalent crowd, both candid and secretive, especially about the strong feelings and actions of love and aggression, eros and violence, just as their knowledge of sex revealed both remarkable openness to science and to medicine as well as a resistant prejudice about sexual bodies (Gay 1984, 3–17).

In its most recent phase—the postmodern period, from about the last half of the twentieth century to today—studies of the culture of emotions have pointed to changes in the standards and styles of emotional expression ("emotionology") and "emotion management," cultures that exert pressures on individuals to curtail emotional intensity. Today's culture of emotions also warns against emotional intensity and extols being and acting "cool," even as it fosters pursuits of pleasure and release (P. Stearns 1994; Bell 1996).

LOCATING TODAY'S EMOTIONAL CULTURE

In a 1989 essay, written for a collection of papers on the new "emotion studies" in sociology, the distinguished US social psychologist Guy Swanson argued that this new field was broader than the designation "emotions" suggested. Its subject matter also concerned values and attitudes, motives and motivations. Swanson identified what a social psychology of human motives and motivations would include: the nature of values and their relation to human motivation and action, the dynamics of arousal, the processes of being satisfied (including experiences of catharsis), "consummations" and fulfillments. His essay is a compendium of the complex and diverse aspects of emotion and emotional experience. But it is also punctuated with metatheoretical reflections and asides about the study of motives and emotions in both classical and contemporary works of psychology and social science, like this one in the essay's conclusion about how the social meaning of "strong feelings" for investigators has recently changed (Swanson 1989, 22–3):

> Until recently, social psychologists tended to treat strong feelings of all sorts as dangerous ... the madness of crowds; the illusions of romantic love; the destructiveness of anger ... Or strong feelings

[shame, guilt, fear] were valued because they forced people to avoid dangers ... The newer studies come from the opposite direction. Values, motives, and motivation provide the "force" that "moves" behavior ... Untamed impulses are celebrated as weapons against personal inauthenticity or the hegemony of an alienating culture ... The right to know one's feelings, and to express them, becomes a criterion of a society fit for people ... Catharsis is studied not only as a process that relieves distress but as often an experience that is sought or generated for its own sake—a kind of savoring of one's situation.

Swanson's reflections, made in 1989, and also found in several early works in the sociology of emotions, concern the current standing of emotions in the academic disciplines and in the culture at large. How and why the emotions today have emerged as important topics of investigation raises other related questions: Why has their place in popular culture grown?[1] What are today's social meanings and messages about emotions and "being emotional"? As Swanson offers his reflections about "today," he looks back at "yesterday." He is, as it were, situating himself (in the late 1980s) at a crossroads of change— change in emotional cultures (or in certain features of today's emotional cultures), one where "strong feelings" were beginning to be rendered in positive terms, as "goods," as sources of something real or authentic, while, at the same time, "too much emotion" was frowned upon. Put differently, "control" and "release" were concurrent cultural preoccupations, as recent studies on this topic have shown (P. Stearns 1994, 1999; cf. Kemper 1990, 3–4).

I want to use Swanson's situation (at the crossroads) as a way of pointing to something about emotional cultures today.[2] By emotional cultures I mean what other social scientists have meant (e.g., Clark 1997; Gordon 1989; Thoits 2004), in particular, the view of emotions as *cultural objects of action, reflection, and management*. By referring to emotions as cultural objects, I mean that they are the *stuff* of human action and signification; cultural objects are anything that human beings can indicate to themselves, including the entire domain of one's own experiences (Blumer 1969; Mead 1934). Cultural objects have a twofold capacity: first, as signifying objects, human agents refer to and act toward them; second, emotions are signs in their own right, they are used to signify something to self or to others. Accordingly, emotions not only serve as objects of elaborate social ritual and interpersonal exchange, emotions also serve as signs of who and what we are, as things we handle and display in our presentation of self, with various degrees of competency and refinement, ability or disability (Thoits 1985, 1990, 2004).

As I address the issue of today's emotional cultures, my inquiry is concerned with both situating today's emotional cultures and identifying their most salient features. My particular point of view—that of a sociologist—is in its discursive (cultural) and structural (institutional) sources: *what are its sociocultural moorings in postmodernity?* While this question may sound either too general or too ambitious to tackle, my aim in this chapter is actually more focused: *to trace how emotion and feeling have become linked to modern identity over time; how emotions have come to serve as cultural symbols ("touchstones") of one's self and one's identity.*

In stating things in this way, I am problematizing what is already a point of agreement among several writers in emotion studies, *the conjunction of emotion and postmodern identity.* That is, I am trying to trace some of the cultural and institutional features of postmodernity that might help us to understand how identity today—an "ideal type" and a feature of today's emotional culture—developed over time. Those who have already pointed to the "emotional self" of postmodernity have argued that the conjunction of emotion and identity is a feature of a distinct emotional culture, an everyday understanding (a "vernacular" speech form) like "the tendency to represent emotion as the foundation and authentication of experiences of self" (Barbalet 1998, 171–2; cf. Baumeister 1986, ch. 11). Or, as Lupton (1998, 6) described today's emotional cultures:

our concepts of our emotions are often integral to our wider conception of our selves; [they are] used to give meaning and provide explanation for our lives, for why we respond to life events, other peoples, material artifacts and places in certain ways, why we might tend to follow patterns of behavior throughout our lives.

In Reddy's (2001, 315) account of our Western "commonsense conceptions of self," emotion is the self's "constitutive feature ... Like thought, memory, intention, or language, emotion is something the self has by virtue of being a self and without which it would not be a self." It is precisely that conception of emotion as something the self *has* that I wish to examine as peculiar to phases of modern identity and its emotional culture, a dominant view of thought and feeling as "possessions of the individual" (Taylor 1985, 277); thinking and feeling are "interiorized"; they are *mine* as is personhood itself. But I also mean by *having* emotions (and "being emotional") that emotions are some of the most important ways that selves search for and discover their authenticity, *who they really are*. Feeling deeply and intensely alive—these are moments and experiences that say to us, "This is *me*! This is who I *really* am!" (Erikson 1968, 19).

However, unlike those authors who have described the self-emotion nexus in postmodernity, my own approach for understanding this coupling is based on two key assumptions: first, the (uncontestable) idea that emotional cultures change; and, second, the idea that integral to changes in emotional cultures are accompanying changes in the *types of identity* or *notions of personhood* that both accompany these changes and produce further changes in culture, identity, and in emotional experiences themselves. Of course, my second assumption is certainly not a new idea in the social and historical sciences. The idea that phases of modern history correspond to changes in *concepts of the person*, in "character," in "identity," and so forth already form a vast literature on "modern individualism" and "national character," as well as of critiques of this tradition by postmodern writers.[3] However, there have been few attempts to examine the emotional features of today's postmodern identity, to examine how—through a reading of works on the shaping of modern identities—emotions (the experiences and the meanings of these experiences) undergo changes too. It might even be argued that where the emotions are concerned, *how the self is construed* matters a great deal. "The bearers of emotion," Barbalet writes, "are always individual persons who experience themselves as being or possessing a self ... The sense of what is meant by emotion derives from experiences of the self" (1998, 187). But what emotions *mean* not only derives from experiences of the self, it also derives from my identity: who I *really* am (whatever that "really" refers to), *how* the self is construed, *what* it believes itself to be, *how* it is connected (or not connected) to other selves, whether or not it *believes* in its own individuality or whether it believes that its individuality is a fiction, whether it can listen to its heart, and so on. All of these aspects of identity as well as others, are closely related to what I mean here by emotional culture.

Here as I portray certain features of today's emotional culture and some of the changes it has undergone, my working assumption is that integral to changes in emotional cultures have been changes in identity, in character, and in the prevailing notions of the self. In advancing this claim, I will be drawing together two related bodies of work: the first on modern identities and the second on the modern history of emotions, two fields that have developed in relative independence of each other. This argument will become clearer through the expositional materials contained in the chapters that follow. For the present, my interest will be to examine a number of studies of postmodern identity in order to propose how emotions and modern identity have been linked and when this linkage occurred.

Returning to Guy Swanson's point about the salience of "strong emotions" in early sociological works on emotions, I am suggesting that the social meanings of "strong emotions"—what they signify and disclose and, especially, what it means to *have* them—are, in important ways, related to postmodern identity, an identity where "our emotions are that which we most deeply espouse as our own" and where our strong emotions reveal to us our most deeply felt hopes and possessions (Reddy 2001, 316). Speaking another way about "identity," we "have very strong feelings about [our] feelings."[4] As Carol Stearns and Peter Stearns (1986) point out in this regard, what we think about our emotions ("emotionology") and our responses to emotions (our own emotions and others' emotions too) can operate to change the emotional experiences themselves. More precisely, *emotional cultures (standards, values, proscriptions, practices, etc.) are part of the emotional experiences themselves.* This way of conceptualizing "culture" and "emotion" has been employed, most effectively, by two recent histories of emotion (C. Stearns and P. Stearns 1986; P. Stearns 2004), as well as by a leading philosopher of emotion (Solomon 1997: 296–7; cf. 2004).

> Emotions . . . are a species of judgment . . . To say that emotions are judgments is to say that they are modes of construal, ways of viewing and engaging the world, including, sometimes, ways of construing the self . . . To say that emotions are "ideational" is not to render them abstract, detached, and lifeless but, to the contrary, to indicate just how energetic and lively ideas can be.

I would like to think that my own argument is an extension of some of these earlier statements about emotion and cognition (or, emotion and judgment), in particular, my claim that emotion studies need to consider "identity" as part of emotional culture itself. This brings to emotion studies a greater sense of the history of selves—of character, of identity, of the person—as *itself* part of the dynamics of changes in emotional cultures. Surely, the fact that "history" and change are central to what modern societies are is closely related to the types of human beings that were produced by those societies and whose actions, with each generation, brought about further changes in those societies. In other words, the profound changes that form part of our modernity narratives—the dissolution of the medieval world, the rise of industrial capitalism, the development of the modern nation-state, the rise of modern sciences and technologies—have had *something* to do with the kinds of persons and identities that were integral to modernity's development. As described by Karl Mannheim ([1924] 1952, 84), it is the dizzying apprehension of our worlds and ourselves as "potentialities, constantly in flux, moving from some point in time to another" that operates on the horizon of our consciousness. In fact, as inhabitants of the modern and postmodern world, it is our destiny and our burden that identities and personalities "take on the fluid and open forum of this society" (Berman 1982, 95). Accordingly, modern "identity" has referred, among other things, to the perception that people's lives and identities are *themselves* processes of active, intervention, choice, and transformation (Giddens 1991, 29). These forms of identity clearly affect how and what "emotions" and "feelings" mean and "say" to modern and post-modern selves in their/our quest "to live an individual life" (Luhmann 1986, 318).

The relative absence of any discussions of the historicity of the "subject" or "human agent," its forms of perception and its prevailing notions of personhood, has severely limited many contemporary studies of changing emotional cultures. In otherwise important studies of the historicity of emotions and emotional cultures, it is remarkable that the shape of the human self or person has been exempted from these histories and that the self that perceives, experiences, and judges those experiences has remained a structure relatively untouched by the "history" to which it is subject and which it produces and reproduces. It is as if a perennial agent or social actor processes the materials—about the social meanings of experiences and emotions—remains untouched by the materials it processes. It is as if *how persons construe themselves* has mattered little when social scientists examine cognition and emotion. But, of course, this construal matters a great deal. In fact, it has been suggested (Marcus and Fisher 1986, 45; cf. C. Geertz [1983] 2000b) that *cultures differ most from one another in the ways they conceive of personhood*: "the grounds of human capabilities and actions, ideas about the self, and the expression of emotions." "Focusing on the person, the self, and the emotions ... is a way of getting to the level at which cultural differences are most deeply rooted: in feelings and in complex indigenous reflections about the nature of persons and social relationships" (Marcus and Fisher 1986, 46).

The type of change in emotional cultures I will try to configure—one where emotional change is a feature of changes of personhood—brings to mind a 1924 essay by Virginia Woolf about the importance of "human character" in writing fiction. That essay, "Mr. Bennett and Mrs. Brown," also contains an argument concerning the remarkable changes in the British novel in the years between the wars, a time preceded by a great change in human character itself. This profound change, Woolf argues, was a change inscribed in the books and the plays of the time (e.g., the books of Samuel Butler and the plays of Bernard Shaw), but also recorded in the "character of one's cook" ([1924] 1984, 194–5):

> The Victorian cook lived like a leviathan in the lower depths,
> formidable, silent, obscure, inscrutable; the Georgian cook is
> a creature of sunshine and fresh air; in and out of the drawing room,
> now to borrow the *Daily Herald*, now to ask advice about a hat.
> Do you ask for more solemn instances of the power of the human
> race to change? Read the *Agamemnon*, and see whether, in process
> of time, your sympathies are not almost entirely with
> Clytemnestra. Or consider the married life of the Carlyles [in
> *The Way of All Flesh*] and bewail the waste ... All human relations
> have shifted—those between masters and servants, husbands and
> wives, parents and children. And when human relations change
> there is at the same time a change in religion, conduct, politics, and
> literature. Let us agree to place one of these changes about
> the year 1910.

Woolf's famous remark that "on or about December, 1910, human character changed" ([1924] 1984, 194) is an assertion she returns to throughout the essay. It is both a remark placed to provoke and startle the listener (The essay was originally written and read as a talk.), as much as to portray a sense of the sudden break with the past that modernity represents: Irving Howe reads Woolf's remark as a hyperbole about modernity: a recognition of the "frightening discontinuity between the traditional past and the shaken present ... The line of history has been bent, perhaps broken."[5] In much the same way that Woolf used this aphorism—"human character changed"—to point to changes in the *new novel* (a novel more interested in human character in itself), my own investigations into today's emotional culture will take me into discussions of the "self" or the "person"—those particular types of beings today who *have* these emotional lives, who pursue certain kinds of emotional experiences, and who think and talk as much as they (we) do about feelings and emotions.

NARRATIVES OF MODERN IDENTITY

"Not 'raw facts' but constructed *stories* sit in the core of virtually all of our social theories."

Margaret R. Somers and Gloria D. Gibson (1994)

"Discourse about identity seems in some important sense distinctively modern—seems, indeed, intrinsic to and partially defining of the modern era."

Craig Calhoun (1994)

I. Modernity and Identity

In what follows, I take up the question of modern identity. As I enter these conversations about the nature of the person in the modern world—conversations coextensive with the history of modernity itself and for which there appears to be no end—I am forced to be selective. For narratives about identity are part of an even larger discourse of "modernity," forming a body of work that extends from classical modernist writers like Tocqueville and Marx to contemporary critics of this discourse as "meta-narrative," Lyotard, Foucault, and Derrida. I regard both of these commentaries (the well-known debates on modernism and postmodernism) as part of the same discourse on modern identity and, like Calhoun

(1991a, 1991b) and Luhmann (1998), I accept the ambiguities of addressing this topic from within modernity or, more accurately, what I call here postmodernity, the period covering the last half of the twentieth century through the present. And while there can be neither a single authoritative nor a final account of what modernity is and has been—such is the ethos of modernity—as moderns, we are fated to observe and to describe what we see and how we see it from where we stand today.

The status of this enterprise, relative to the narratives of modernity it addresses, is conversational and interpretative. This means, among other things, that this is a discussion from within the world it is describing. This assertion also means that my attempt to describe something about emotions today shows us something about ourselves by "fixing" it long enough for us to look at it and to recognize ourselves in its description. Here I draw from Clifford Geertz ([1973] 2000a, 20): "The interpreting involved consists in trying to rescue the 'said' of such discourse from its perishing occasions and fix it in perusable terms." The project of fixing "identity," of course, also engages me in choices about what these ideas about the "modern" mean. In the broadest sense and for my purposes here, my understanding is a cultural understanding: *modernist culture (to which "identity" belongs) refers to change and discontinuity in all dimensions of social life: "The [modern] world is in a rush."*[6]

But my principal concern here is change within the realm of "subjectivity," ideas and practices about what persons are and what their experiences mean— particularly their experiences *about themselves.* Modernist culture opens up the self to change, restlessness, and volatility. *Subjectivity* is its unquestioned point of view. Its disposition is *inwardness.* My attempt here is to recount some of the ways that modern identity's history has been narrated. In framing the problem of modern identity this way—within narratives—I am intentionally drawing together the narratives of identity of sociological theories and those historical actors they describe. Narrative and narrativity are concepts of both "social epistemology" (social theories of knowing) and "social ontology" (the being of historical actors) (Somers and Gibson 1994, 58–9):

> It is through narrativity that we come to know, understand, and make sense of the social world, and it is through narratives and narrativity that we constitute our social identities ... It matters not whether we are social scientists or subjects of historical research for all of us come to be who we are (however, ephemeral, multiple, and changing) by locating ourselves (usually unconsciously) in social narratives *rarely of our own making.*

In classic texts of social theory, the special nature of the problem of identity within modernity has been discussed by differentiating itself ("modern identity") relative to its own temporal past ("ancient" vs. "modern," "traditional" vs. "modern"). In fact, this feature of its discourse opens up something of the nature of "identity" itself, whether that of persons or entire societies: the differentiation of "self-reference" and "external reference" (Luhmann 1998, 3). Put differently, "identity turns on the interrelated problems of self-recognition and recognition by others" (Calhoun 1994, 20): an identity is known and asserted relative to the other—whether individual or group, the present relative to the past, the self relative to the other, or ruler relative to subject: I discover what it is to be an American as an American abroad (James Baldwin, 1959); I confront what it is to be an African-American through the rebuffs of a white classmate (W. E. B. DuBois, [1903] 1994). Identity inescapably involves this contradiction: in the social experiences I share with others, I come to know my own identity and individuality. For self-consciousness is characterized by an ability to arouse in oneself the response of another; self-knowledge and identity entail *self-objectification*—a process of discovering one's own otherness (a me-ness) in a world of others, a consciousness that the self sweeps into its own field of experience (Crapanzano 1992, 79; Mead 1934, 138).[7]

According to classical social theory, the "master-narrative of modernity" (Somers and Gibson 1994), the modern world was a social formation whose main features were set against "traditional society"—whether in Marx's account of the exploitation of capitalist wage labor, Durkheim's on the industrial division of labor, or Weber's portrait of the "rationalization" of the West. Modern identity meant the *release* of social actors from the confines of traditionalism. Accordingly, the familiar contours of modern identity—individuality, isolation, inwardness, dislocation, crisis—form a distinct *vocabulary* of the modern self, one embedded in this master-narrative.

In much the same way that Raymond Williams in *Culture and Society* ([1958] 1983) examined words (a "vocabulary," he called it) that first came into their present usage in the decades 1780 to 1850 ("industry," "democracy," "culture," etc.), one can propose a distinct vocabulary of the self—words, phrases, but also metaphors—that we use to narrate modern identity. In the same spirit that marked Williams's inquiry in his later book *Keywords* ([1976] 1985, 15), I attempt here to record today's (and yesterday's) vocabulary of the self or the person (see also Burgett and Hendler 2007):

> It is not a series of ... definitions ... It is, rather, the record of an inquiry into a *vocabulary*: a shared body of words and meanings in our most general discussions, in English ... They are significant, binding words in certain activities and their interpretations; they are significant, indicative words in certain forms of thought.

2. The Problem of Identity

> "Modern man is afflicted with a *permanent identity crisis*, a condition conducive to considerable nervousness."
> Peter L. Berger, Brigitte Berger, and Hansfried Kellner (1973)

> "Identity ... the more one writes about this subject, the more the word becomes a term for something as unfathomable as it is all-pervasive."
> Erik Erikson (1968)

"Identity," a keyword of modernity in its contemporary phrase, carries the weight and the burden of moral significance; it evokes a need—for a sense of self; it imposes tasks—self-actualization, negotiation, choice; it points to struggles we are obliged to undergo or to suffer—identity crises; it reveals inevitabilities of self-change in a world of change. In these senses and others, identity has been invested with intellectual and moral significance (Gleason 1983, 911) by both professionals (psychologists, therapists, counselors) and laypersons. In popular culture—print, film, television—there is a widespread interest in the self, its identity crises, its successes and failures of self-esteem and self-fulfillment. Identity is a road on which anyone who is anyone is supposed to be traveling. And unlike that yellow brick road, we expect that there is no Wizard at its end pointing out the way. Identity is supposed to be entirely in one's own hands.

Among academics who write about identity and the social self, it has been effectively argued that problems of the "self" (self-awareness, self-presentation, self-schemas, self-monitoring, self-concepts, to mention some of these) constitute one of the major topics of modern psychology (Baumeister 1987a). And while "identity" is central to social psychological theory and research (Howard 2000), it has broken through the restrictive confines of any single academic discipline and is a topic addressed across the humanities and social sciences (Hollinger 1997; Appiah and Gates 1995; Lash and Friedman 1992). In fact, the proliferation of writings and debates on "identities" across the disciplines can itself be seen as a register of the ways that *subjectivity, self,* and *individual* form a subject matter without end, one inherited from modern social theory (1890–1930). There, modernity's "individual" emerged with the breakup of feudal society: when the ("rational" and technical) forces of industrialization unleashed themselves on modernity's "societies" and "communities," the individual emerged as *itself* part of this progressive movement, according to one of the dominant narratives of modernity: the individual was freed from traditional ties, and, in time, became fully "individuated," a being separate and apart, a unique person or entity, yet integral to a species or a group (R. Williams [1958] 1983, 164–5).

To understand "how the self became a problem," as the psychologist Baumeister (1987a) has framed this, is to ask about its emergence as a cultural object of immense social significance. This is, of course, a historical question. It is also a cultural question about changes in *ideas* and *practices* about subjectivity, about the lives and destinies of individuals as told in the emerging identity narratives of modernity (novels, autobiographies, philosophical and psychological texts and treatises, diaries).

To begin to describe today's *vocabulary of the self* is to begin with the emergence of self *as a problem* and a preoccupation—a problem at once intellectual and discursive as well as everyday, part of the quotidian, the knowledge and experience of everyday life. The social and intellectual histories that address this problem are remarkably compatible, whether those of a psychologist (Baumeister 1987a, 1987b, 1991), a literary critic (Trilling 1971), a sociologist of knowledge (Berger 1963, 1970, a sociologist of art and culture (R. Williams 1961), a historical sociologist (Elias [1939] 2000, 2001), or social philosophers (Gehlen 1980; Taylor 1989), to name some of the academic disciplines I draw from in this discussion. In these texts—however differently stated and argued—the idea (and associated cultural and political practices) of the "individual" develops as itself part of the history of modern thought and life. In this development, the individual self—its mind, its emotions, its identity—becomes a subject of debate and discussion without end.

In his studies, in words and language, of the development of a distinctly modern vocabulary ("culture," "society," "economy"), Raymond Williams provides an account of the first uses of "an individual" and later "the individual" in the English language of the late eighteenth century; these words describe "a fundamental order of being," and in the course of the nineteenth century, he notes, there is "a remarkable efflorescence of the word" (R. Williams [1976] 1985, 163–4). This new word and idea develop alongside of "individuality" and "individualism" (Swart 1962; cf. Lukes 1973). Williams's project ([1976] 1985, 22) rests on the argument that some socially significant processes "occur *within* language," in the introduction of new words and in the adopting and changing of older words and usages.[8]

As to the arguments and accounts of the historical and cultural emergence of "the individual," Williams's brief statement is emblematic ([1976] 1985, 163–4):

> The emergence of notions of individuality, in the modern sense, can be related to the break-up of the medieval social, economic, and religious order. In the general movement against feudalism there was a new stress on a man's personal existence over and above his place or function in a rigid hierarchical society. There was a related stress, in Protestantism, on a man's direct and individual relation to God, as opposed to this relation [mediated] by the Church.

Baumeister's account also uses the images and ideas of unity/disunity, location/dislocation (1987a, 171); his formulation of the primacy of "attitudes" is in keeping with his psychological perspective.

> The relation of self to society became a problem when ... two basic attitudes were destroyed ... The first ... by the rise in social mobility, which detached the individual from [one's] social station ... and by the growth of internality ... The second ... as humanity ceased to live by Christian faith and imagery ...
> The second attitude was also undermined by the fact that society gradually ceased giving each person an unequivocal message about how to live and what to do.

Another influential formulation concerning the social changes that led to a distinctly modern identity structure comes from the sociologist Peter Berger and his coauthors Brigitte Berger and Hansfried Kellner. In their description of modern "pluralization" and its effects on modern "identity," the authors present the argument that modern identity is "peculiarly open and ... differentiated" (1973, 77–8).[9]

> Because of the plurality of social worlds in modern society, the structures of each particular world are experienced as relatively

unstable and unreliable ... The individual's experience of himself becomes more real to him than his experience of the objective social world ... If this is coupled with ... [openness], the crisis of modern identity becomes manifest ... The individual's main foothold in reality ... is constantly changing. Consequently it should not be a surprise that modern man is afflicted with a *permanent identity crisis*, a condition conducive to considerable nervousness.

Craig Calhoun (1994, 11–12), writing of the "break-up" of kinship and other "all-encompassing identity scheme[s]," offers a compatible argument:

> Modernity has meant in significant part the break-up—or the reduction to near-irrelevance—of most all-encompassing identity schemes. Kinship still matters to us as individuals; we invest it with great emotional weight, but kinship no longer offers us an overall template of social and personal identities ... The modern era brought an increase in the multiplicity of identity schemes so substantial that it amounted to a qualitative break ... In the modern era, identity is always constructed and situated in a field and amid a flow of contending cultural discourses.

To recapitulate, various accounts—authoritative within the human sciences—understand modern identity as a problem due to changing configurations of "society" or "social structure," beginning in the early modern period and developing during the various phases of modern history. These accounts focus on the ways that people *experienced themselves* (and were experienced by others), as part of a community or group ("traditional society"). Modern "individuals" increasingly come to see themselves as independent of or separate from groups or "society." For example, in one of the earliest accounts by Burckhardt ([1890] 1954, 100): "man was conscious of himself only as a member of a race, people, party, family, or corporation," while in the Renaissance "man became a spiritual *individual*, and recognized himself as such." Similarly, in Tocqueville's ([1840] 1990, 98–9) influential account of individualism, he makes this contrast: aristo-cratic society attaches people to something "strongly marked and permanent," larger than themselves; this is replaced by democratic individualism, an attachment to oneself and one's little circle.

In these accounts, the transition from traditional medieval communities to modern societies is marked by a growing complexity ("differentiation," "pluralization") of societies, communities, and people's life-worlds.[10]

These changes, in particular, help to explain how modern "individuals," in comparison with their predecessors, are no longer closely integrated within a social world and how this leads to modern ideas and ideologies of the "autonomous individual." Put differently, modernity means the weakening ("breakup," "dislocation") of the great stabilizing and integrating forces of human existence, both tradi-tional communities as well as the cultural systems of religion and kinship. As a result, people's lives are less and less determined, in an all-encompassing way, by these social forces and are increasingly understood as "personal" and "individual" states, interests, or projects: "The emergence of notions of 'individuality,' in the modern sense, can be related to the break-up of the medieval social, economic and religious order" (R. Williams [1976] 1985, 163). It is in this sense too that Luhmann (1998, 4) understands modernity to be "a release of individuality" and that Gehlen (1980) describes modern "subjectivi-zation" as a social psychological response to the experienced loss of stable institutions.

As I have described it here, the "problem of modern identity" refers to the emergence of the problem of one's *standing* or *location* in the social order: because of the changes that mark every feature of the modern world (political, economic, communal), the question of a person's identity arises as *itself* part of the configuration of the modern world. To recapitulate, the problem of modern identity is as much a problem of belonging, continuity (sameness) as it is a problem of place (community, status, etc.) within a social world marked by change, mobility, and discontinuity. These problems are imposed both on persons by the social and collective conditions of the modern world and on modern individuals *themselves*. For modern societies are made up of (self-defining) individuals who must navigate the complex world of modern societies and their various institutional sectors. Individuals are also burdened with the problem of their identities: *people's lives and identities are increasingly perceived as processes of active intervention, choice, and transformation* (Berman 1982, 1992; Giddens 1991). That is, the matter of one's identity is not a matter resolved once and for all. Rather, it is a (subjective) reality that must be continually readdressed. As a number of contemporary writers have argued, identities today develop relative to a self-concept of change: a mutable self (Zurcher 1977), a self-as-tourist (Bauman 1996), a homeless self (Berger, Berger, and Kellner 1973). And no matter how fully people *commit* to their identities, these identities are, in fact, both multiple and changing (Swaan 1997). In fact, the very idea of a "commitment" to an identity (like a commitment to a partnership or a marriage) suggests a process characterized by volatility: in such an environment there arises a need to engage this identity (or this person) over that one, at least for now. Talk of commitment belies a surrender to "choice" in a world where nothing is permanent. In fact, identity itself has been portrayed as an escape— more neutrally, an imposed choice one makes—in the face of inevitable uncertainties (Bauman 1996, 19):

> One thinks of identity whenever one is not sure of where one belongs; that is, one is not sure how to place oneself among the evident variety of behavioral styles and patterns, and how to make sure that people around would accept this placement as right and proper, so both sides would know how to go on in each other's presence. "Identity" is a name given to the escape sought from that uncertainty.[11]

Among the various accounts presented here, modern life is portrayed ("narrated") as a condition of permanent change, also characterized as dislocation, breakup, fragmentation, isolation.

Indeed, these are the terms used in several of the accounts above. It is an account that is as much *about society* as it is *about individuals*. For the changes brought about by the new industrial societies—in the nature of work as in kinship and religion—were changes that transformed social life and, in turn, reverberated in the lives of individuals, changing people themselves into "individuals." It is an account identified with the naturalistic vision of the sociologist Emile Durkheim, especially in *The Division of Labor in Society* ([1893] 1984, 400):

> As we advance in the evolutionary scale, the ties which bind the individual to his family, to his native soil, to traditions which the past has given him, to collective group usages, become loose. More mobile, he changes his environment more easily, leaves his people to go elsewhere to live a more autonomous existence, to a greater extent forms his own ideas and sentiments.

Central to Durkheim's naturalistic portrait of modern individuals ("as we advance . . . ") is the theme that has marked virtually all classical accounts of modern identity and individuality—the liberal theme arising in eighteenth-century political treatises of personal "autonomy," the greater "individuality" and freedom of modern selves relative to both their societies and their (traditional) predecessors. Despite extensive and lengthy critiques of "autonomy" in modern academic disciplines from philosophy to linguistics, aimed both at its ontology and its sociopolitical consequences, this individualist image of the autonomous, self-determining individual prevails in virtually all domains of contemporary US society and its cultural practices. It may, in fact, be thought of as the principal signifier of our "freedom" and emancipation—a freedom that we Americans seek to continually achieve. In D. H. Lawrence's words, the United States is a republic of "escaped slaves," a nation of "the masterless;" in "breaking away from all dominion," we are our own masters (McClay 1994). In a related text, James Jasper (2000) discusses the American fascination with movement and reinvention.

3. Autonomous Individuals

One of the hallmarks of modern identity, "autonomy," is not so much a word in the emerging everyday life and culture of modernity, as it is a word in the vocabulary of those modern elites and intellectuals whose ideas both reflected and shaped our ideas of what "modernity" is (Hughes 1958); most notably, in Kant's ethical theory an autonomous agent can direct its actions by its (autonomous) will, a concern that addressed how—when freed from political and religious authorities—human beings can rule themselves and engage in "moral self governance" (Schneewind 1998, 1986). For Voltaire, Diderot, and Rousseau "autonomy" was articulated as actions against political and religious authorities and against tradition; autonomy meant freedom from domination.

While "autonomy," from its first uses in the seventeenth century, has not been in ordinary people's speech—even today it operates as part of academic and scientific discourse—"autonomy" reflects a far more widespread cultural experience. It is, in Keith Oatley's (2004, 16–17) words, a "piece of folk theory," a pretheoretical or preconscious idea that we draw from to understand ourselves and our worlds. Accordingly, as folk theory, autonomy means a *valuing* of the sense of our separation from others and from society itself, a sense that if our destinies are not in our own hands, they should be. Autonomy also refers to people's experiences of themselves as relatively independent beings, as centers of knowledge and consciousness, as vital sources of action. This is what modern selfhood *is*: modern societies are "individualistic" insofar as the actions of individual persons are among their preeminent values (Meyer 1986, 209):

> [Modern] society is itself rationalized as rooted in the behavior and choices of individuals and as functioning for their benefit; it is, as it were, not quite sacred itself but rather the product of its sacred individual members. It is justified, not by its history, but by the extent to which it benefits the individuals who are both its ultimate producers and its ultimate consumers.

As this statement clearly indicates, individual autonomy is an idea embedded in early modern political and economic texts and treatises: individual *freedom* and *autonomy* are ideas about the newly emerging markets and nation-states of industrial capitalism, where persons are configured as independent (autonomous) and self-sufficient social actors vis-à-vis "society" and other individuals. "Individuals" were, among other things (and they were *many* things), integral and indispensable to modern free markets and nation-states, their organizations and their logics; this was, of course, what Karl Marx understood as the *ideology* embedded in the theories of Adam Smith and David Ricardo, so vital to the entire fabric of bourgeois society, an ideology that conceived of the individual not as *the product of the dissolution of feudal society* but as the "starting point of history," both an ideal and something "posited by nature." As Marx recounts, it was during this epoch—the period of modern bourgeois history—that this isolated and autonomous individual was *produced*. It was an idea developed within the leading sociopolitical narratives of modernity; it is an idea about *ruling* just as it is an idea about identity, *who* rules. Autonomous individuals formed the units of the new and developing political economy of capitalist nation-states, or so they were construed and idealized (Barbalet 1998,172ff.).[12] Similarly, the modern political idea of the "social contract" was based on the idea of the primacy of individual consciousness (Heller, Sosna, and Wellbery, 1986, 5).

> The agreement of presocial, autonomous subjects to better their
> autarchic existences by cooperative interaction remains the
> ideological core of the contemporary Western political economy.

Again, this is not to claim that political and economic theories are the only or even the principal sites of early modern individualism. For individual autonomy and freedom are not reducible to any single discursive source, nor is this "monumental change in self-understanding," to which I have been referring, solely "discursive" (Taylor 1989, 199): autonomy and freedom

have been be traced to multiple discursive and institutional sites
and practices: to Renaissance humanism, Reformation theology, as
well as to the developing capitalist economy, its historical subjects
as well as its sociological narratives about "modernization."[13]
Which is to say that *the individual* is an emergent figure in modern
doctrine, dogma, social and political treatise, autobiography, and so
forth; *this* individual is conceived as a *center of consciousness*, not
the product but the origin and foundation of social life and
institutions.

In fact, it is important to note that the claims (among them, my
own) concerning the social and discursive histories of the modern
individual as a social *construct*, stands in opposition—as a counter
discourse—to the very idea of individual *autonomy* (independence,
ability to freely act and to choose) where free and autonomous persons
are *not* to be identified with anything fashioned by the forces of the
"social," not the product of some external order. In fact, the very
meaning of "individual" or "individuality" means the person who
I am, *irrespective* of the social roles I occupy and the functions
I perform: I am a person "in my own right"; that is, the modern
description of the individual means "a kind of absolute, without
immediate reference" to the various groups of which I am a member.
Raymond Williams (1961, 73–4) dates this meaning of the individual
to England in the late sixteenth and early seventeenth century, giving
as its most likely source Reformation ideas about the individual soul:
in Protestant thinking, the *relationship* of a person's soul with God is
direct and personal.[14] For faith and salvation are no longer understood
as occurring through the mediating function of the Church and its
sacraments. The relationships within which one's faith and salvation
take place undergo remarkable changes, from a hierarchical and
communal set of relationships to a relationship that is understood as
direct (unmediated): one's faith is discovered in the solitude of one's
soul before God, such as in Luther's "priesthood of the believer."
"Autonomy," then, also refers to the Reformation's freeing of
conscience, the making of modern individual conscience, and

a newly emerging notion of the self as an "inner self," a topic I will address shortly.

Which is to say that this modern idea of an *inner self* also has a history, one that has been traced in recent works by the philosopher Charles Taylor (1989) and by the psychologist Roy Baumeister (1986). Both have written very different treatises on modern identity. Despite these differences, they have given central treatment to the modern understanding of identity as an *inner self*. It is from these accounts that I will draw in my attempt to assemble a portrait of modern inwardness. Of all the texts on identity treated here, the quality of *inwardness* bears most directly on our understanding of today's emotional self.

4. Contours of the Modern Subject: Inwardness

At whatever moment we enter the history of modern selfhood or "modern individualism"— with nineteenth-century accounts of modern bourgeois individualism or with its beginnings in Renaissance humanism, what Burckhardt ([1890] 1954) called the development of the free or "spiritual individual," or more recently with Freud's monumental creation of its interior topography—we discover in this process something new and distinctive in the human person, its *inwardness*. By "inwardness," I do not mean what philosophers call self-consciousness, that universal ability to distinguish ourselves and our own experiences from others and from our worlds; nor do I mean the reflexive quality of human thought and speech where, in thinking and in speaking, one's thought and speech become part of a deliberate and conscious repertoire inserted into human relations and intercourse. To claim that only modern persons can be so characterized is to deny to all but a few what is clearly a mark of us all: *we are universally signifying beings, both reflective and dialogical.*

The meaning of inwardness I wish to convey is a disposition— moral, spiritual, and psychological—one that in modern societies has come to be viewed as a *social good*. To be a self, according to modern cultural meanings, involves persons in the pursuit and acquisition of self-knowledge, a knowledge not for its own sake but for the purpose of controlling and "fashioning" one's selfhood or identity, for making up oneself, for articulating one's own presence in the world. "Self-fashioning," as Greenblatt (1980, 1) calls it, is not an invention of modernity; there were selves and "a sense that they could be fashioned" before this era. But what *was* born in the early modern era of the sixteenth century was both an "increased self-consciousness about the fashioning of human identity as a manipulable, artful process" and a newfound sense of autonomy: "The power to impose a shape upon oneself is an aspect of the more general power to control identity—that of others at least as often as one's own" (Greenblatt 1980,1–2; cf. Elias [1939] 2000, 85–109).

This inwardness is also a disposition that has attached us, relative to other peoples and civilizations, to *ourselves*, an argument made first by Tocqueville ([1840] 1990) in his chapter on "democratic individualism." Durkheim elaborated it later, and more systematically, in his study of the industrial division of labor. What Taylor, in his recent work on modern identity, construes as the modern disposition of *inwardness* was itself a theme of modern sociological narratives of the individual. As Durkheim ([1893] 1984, 122) noted with his characteristic concern for "social solidarity," the modern *cult of the individual* turned people inward:

> There is indeed one area in which the [modern] common [collective] consciousness has grown stronger ... in its view of the individual. As all the other beliefs and practices assume less and less religious a character, the individual becomes the object of a sort of religion. We carry on the worship of the dignity of the human person which, like all strong acts of worship, has already acquired its superstitions ... It is indeed from society that it draws all its strength, but it is not to society that it binds us: it is to ourselves.

This disposition has also given to the domain of the "subjective" and "personal" decidedly emotional social values—values of sentiment: the modern self is directed to a field of new objects—objects that exist in a new social space, a world of *inner objects*, [Charles Taylor's term (1989)], objects whose meaning and significance hardly existed before the seventeenth century, that age of sentimentalism when modern "subjectivity" and its "culture of interiority" might be traced.[15] Or, as Taylor (1989, 284) argues, with the eighteenth-century theory of the sentiments, feelings and sentiments became "normative," turning the self inward to a domain where nature ("the voice within") speaks to us:

> Sentiment is now important ... because undistorted, normal feeling is my way of access into the design of things, which is the real constitutive good, determining good and bad ... The new place of sentiment completes the revolution which has yielded a modern view of nature as normative, so utterly different from the ancient view ... The modern view ... endorses nature as the source of right impulse or sentiment ... Nature as norm is an inner tendency; it is ready to become the voice within, which Rousseau will make it, and to be transposed by the Romantics into a richer and deeper inwardness.

In *Sources of the Self*, Taylor gives us a history of the "modern identity," by which he means an intellectual history, a tracing—in literature, philosophy, art—of what it means to be a self, "the senses of inwardness, freedom, individuality, and being embedded in nature which are at home in the modern West" (1989, ix). Central to this project is the elaboration of a "massive shift" in the self's valuation of emotions: first, by the eighteenth century there is an entirely new understanding of the "subject" where thoughts and valuations are psychic phenomena—they are *in the mind;* "what was previously seen as existing ... between knower/agent and world, linking them and making them inseparable" (188) is now seen as belonging to the subject. Taylor and others have called this shift "a new subjectivism." "Thought and feeling—the psychological— are now confined to minds" (186).[16]

Secondly, Taylor elaborates this "massive shift" in its corresponding notion of the good—its love of nature and its "cult of sensibility"—and traces its development in philosophical texts, but also other works that trace—in the history of commercial activity, in marriage and family life, in religious movements and revivals (among Pietists and Methodists), and in the rise of the modern novel—changes in sentiments, ethical outlooks, and new understandings about nature's vitality and the importance of "inner life" and feelings as "moral sources" of the modern person. In this way, Taylor documents movements that both reflected and helped to usher in the rise of a modern and individualist culture: it values personal autonomy; it renders "self-exploration" important, particularly the understanding of one's emotions; its "visions of the good life ... involve personal commitment" (Taylor 1989, 285–6).

I am highlighting Taylor's tracing of the history of the modern identity—a person of sentiments and a sentimental person—as a way to describe its important discursive sources; this is an *intellectual* (principally, philosophical) historical study and not a work of "historical explanation," as Taylor himself makes clear. For his project is an interpretive study—inter alia, an account of the making of modern identity, its force in the world, its consequences for the social actors for whom it has operated, its function as moral vision. As a cultural study, its concerns, which are very much my own, also engage questions about how modern identity has found expression in a number of collective practices integral to what is known as "modernity." For these practices entailed new and different self-understandings for economic and political life and, for example, for new religious movements in piety and practice of the Reformation of the early modern period:

> A wide range of practices ... converged and reinforced each other to produce [modern identity]: the practices, for instance, of religious prayer and ritual, of spiritual discipline as a member of a Christian congregation, of self-scrutiny as one of the regenerate, of the politics of consent, of the family life of companionate marriage ... of artistic creation under the demands of originality ... of voluntary

associations, of the cultivation and display of sentiment . . .
(Taylor 1989, 206)[17]

Taylor's idea of the self—one that is clearly different from dominant theories of the self in the social sciences today, yet one resonant
with Durkheim's sociology—is that the self is a being constituted in
the taking of moral positions, of acting relative to "goods," however
differently understood in particular historical and cultural circumstances. His question: *how did modern notions of the good develop
along with new understandings of human agency and selfhood?* I will
return to this question again, for it contains a proposition about the
emotions as powerful cultural objects (McCarthy 1989a, 1989b)
*whose momentum derives from their interior location as natural
forces within, as inner essences.* As many have argued, these inner
essences (emotions) have been with us since the cultural transformations of the seventeenth century and the movements of eighteenth-
century Enlightenment and nineteenth-century Romanticism. Taylor
(1989, 284) describes how it was that sentiments became "normative"
in the eighteenth century and links norms regarding sentiments with
the modern self's inwardness.[18]

Certainly, the emotions have taken on different social meanings
over time, not only expressed in (and expressing) changing discursive
forms, academic writings, print and digital journalism, the speeches of
public figures, everyday knowledges and speech. I am also thinking of
new forms of writing (including the rise of the modern novel) and
graphics, manners of speech, and new types of thought and practice
like psychoanalysis and psychology, and also of changes in the repre-
sentational forms of identity seen in real and fictional heroes and what
we today call "role models." In other words, there is a "vocabulary of
emotion" (H. Geertz 1959) whose history can be traced in the many
forms of representation and writing—a "shared body of words and
meanings . . . significant, binding words in certain activities and their
interpretation" (DeJean 1997, xiii, 91; cf. R. Williams [1976] 1985, 15).
And while we know something of its sources in early modern history—a

history of emotions traced, however differently, by Taylor's (1989) intellectual history of modern inwardness and Reddy's (2001) proposal for a history of emotions, today's emotions belong to a vocabulary of more recent origin whose "key words" might include: self, identity, freedom, authenticity, psychology, pleasure, culture, nature. Taylor's intellectual history of modern inwardness, where feelings and sentiments become both normative and moral signifiers of personhood (Am I a person of deep feelings or a shallow person, even a sociopath?), can be read alongside of Norbert Elias's classic sociological treatise ([1939] 2000; see also Appendix B below) on the changing forms of social controls and self-controls, changes, he argues, that are coextensive with the rise of modernity itself.

Sociologists of emotion claim a variety of classic works as part of their current perspective and set of research problems.[19] Among these works, Norbert Elias's *The Civilizing Process* is singled out for its examination of human emotionality within a framework of social and historical change. The direct relevance of Elias's work to a discussion of modern "inwardness" and its valuation of emotion and feeling is to be found in its argument that the social changes associated with modernity (most especially, greater social differentiation or complexity and the increased interdependencies that coincided with the formation of modern nation-states and their centralization of power) were accompanied by simultaneous changes in the body, its functions, and in the self's capacity for self-consciousness and self-monitoring, with increased levels of shame, embarrassment, and disgust associated with the body and its functions. These changes also coincided with the rise in a distinct *consciousness of self*—an increased sense of "autonomy" and an accompanying experienced separation of the self from the "outside world" (Elias [1939] 2000, 472ff.).[20]

Elias's historical argument is fruitfully read alongside Taylor's treatise on the *discursive* history of modern identity (in philosophy, theology, literature, etc.). For both authors provide a portrait of modern selfhood as a *form* (with an accompanying set of social practices) that has, in time, moved inward. This interior movement—we think of feelings and thoughts and, indeed, our truest selves as "inside" or "within" us—has many sources and expressions: increased social controls on instincts and emotions become internalized; the body and its functions undergo a "civilizing" process that renders this domain private and intimate, certainly embarrassing and, sometimes, shameful; the "civilizing" process coincides, in important ways, with an "increasing split between an intimate and public sphere, between private and public behavior" (Elias [1939] 2000, 160). This divided self is also a self whose interiority is experienced as *nature within us* (Taylor); our "inside" or our interiority is the place where we discover—in sentiment and feeling—not only who we are, but nature itself brimming within us: "The world about us would be desolate except for the world within us."[21]

Elias's argument—that increased social controls corresponded to an increase in personal controls and an accompanying rise in levels of shame and anxiety surrounding the body and its functions—is clearly a sociohistorical argument, despite its resonance with Freudian theory (Elias [1939] 2000, 442, emphasis in original):

> *We realize the degree to which the fears and anxieties that move people are human-made* ... The strength, kind and structure of the fears and anxieties that smoulder or flare in the individual never depend solely on his or her own "nature" ... They are always determined, finally, by the history and the actual structure of his or her relations to other people, by the structure of society; and they change with it.

As Elias argues here, modern history tells us how much culture matters in this process: how the modern disposition or *habitus* is a construct of changes in European (and, later, North American) standards of behavior, standards thrust into social life as sociopolitical interdependencies changed, changes that coincided with modern civilization's development: "The fortunes of a nation over the centuries become sedimented into the habitus of its individual members" (Elias 1996, 19).

This notion of the modern individual as a sealed or closed off monad (evoking Leibnitz), a world-unto-itself, is also discussed by Norbert Elias ([1939] 2000, 471–2) as *homo clausus*:

> The image of the individual as an entirely free, independent being, a "closed personality" who is "inwardly" quite self-sufficient and separate from all other people, has behind it a long tradition in the development of European societies ... The conception of the individual as *homo clausus*, a little world in himself who ultimately exists quite independently of the great world outside, determines the image of human beings in general. Every other human being is likewise seen as a *homo clausus;* his core, his being, his true self appears likewise as something divided within him by an invisible wall from everything outside ... But the nature of this wall itself is hardly ever considered and never properly explained.

Taylor provides an account of inwardness and feelings as meaningful *possessions* of the modern subject. Elias's account completes the picture, as it were, arguing that modern inwardness is an outgrowth of a lengthy and complex psychic formation that entailed increased levels of self-control and self-monitoring accompanied by increased levels of shame, embarrassment, and anxiety surrounding the person and the body as a carefully managed and controlled object or entity existing before the gaze of others and oneself.

In his distinctive account of modern "subjectivization," the social philosopher Arnold Gehlen offers a compatible portrait of the *modern person's inner elaboration*, characterized by unprecedented degrees of psychic awareness, arguing that "never before were so many people equipped with such fine sensors" (1980, 81). The modern novel simultaneously reflects and advances this condition of modern "subjectivization," as does modern psychology and modern art forms. Citing the critic Wilhelm Hausenstein, Gehlen portrays the objective reality of the modern subject as "scattered patches ... residues of things disrupted by the passage of a fast train or a car" (83). The subjective element does not merely "stand above all others ... It is the only one that counts" (as cited in Gehlen 1980, 82); subjectivity is the primary reality in the experience of modern subjects.

Throughout his long career, Elias explored the mental configurations of modern life, particularly the image of *homo clauses*, literally, man-in-a-box, described above. According to Elias's thinking, the individual and society are collective *representations*, images, or perspectives that changed as societies configured persons and collectivities differently: changes take place in the ways that the plurality of persons ("society") is understood, as well as in the ways that individual persons forming societies understand themselves (e.g., as "individuals"); together these make up the *habitus* of individuals and this habitus is a vital element of a people's culture. Both configurations—individual and society—can also be grasped in the ways that they exist relative to each other, what Elias calls the "we-I balance" or the individual identity and the collective identity. One of Elias's arguments is that people in modern societies construe "individual" and "society" as antithetical. But Elias is also interested in studying how, over the last half of the twentieth century, the relationship continued to change (2001, 162ff.). Furthermore, there is continual change over a person's lifespan in how the we-I relation is configured and reconfigured through changing circumstances reflected in memory.

EMOTIONAL LIVES/EMOTIONAL SELVES

It is time for me to bring the preceding discussion of modern identity closer to the topic at hand—the emotions. This also entails bringing the narratives of modern identity up to date. In fact, a number of observers of contemporary (postmodern) culture have noted that ours is a time of emotional overload characterized by a kind of hypersaturation (Gergen 2001), or an "emancipation of emotions" (Wouters 1992), or a "liquid" world (Bauman 2005), where the principal moorings for our identities are the emotions we feel (or try to feel or are told to feel). Emotion "enjoys unprecedented status in the moral life" in a culture where the untrammeled self stands center stage (Taylor 1989, 284; cf. Bell 1996). Emotions today—how did we get here?—are believed to be "the foundation and authenticator of experiences of self" (Barbalet 1998, 172).

If modern identity and its emotional life are a subject matter of near-endless interest to us today, it is a subject matter built on another (modern) idea, namely, that phases of modern history correspond to changes in the concepts of the person, in "character," even in what we call "human nature." And if the continuing narratives about ourselves—postmodern identities—tell us anything, they speak and write in both texts and images of highly emotional and sentimental terms. They are also written as announcements of the end of the modern "subject" or individual; certainly they tell us of the end or waning of the rational self (Enlightenment) or the essential or core or unchanging self—modern culture's central character. For the "individual"— modernity's artifact and maker—has fallen on hard times. This is not only due to the rantings of some about a "culture of narcissism" or the emergence of a "minimal self" (Christopher Lasch)—the contracting of self to a defensive core, armed against society; or the warnings of others (Daniel Bell) that at the heart of "post-industrial culture" lies a culture whose center *is* the self— modernity's untrammeled self, entirely suited up for the consumer society (preferably in jeans by Diesel and underwear by Calvin Klein, if not exactly in that order). Of course these rantings and many more are what we have to endure for having survived modernism and made it into the twenty-first century. In fact, today we are surrounded by gloom-and-doom messages about "the end" ... of civilization, morality, the family, "character," Christianity, whatever. But this is not where I was going, to a message of moral crisis and ending of the world as we know it.

What I mean about the postmodern self's virtual disappearance (and, my students concur in their own matter-of-fact way about this) is that we live today without a belief in an essential self, a deep inner self, a self we seek over the journey of our lives, a truly autonomous individual of which I have spoken. In today's world of everyday life (as well as in the world of the academy) we are more acutely aware than ever, that selves—like the social realities around us—are in change, uprooted, in transit; or, that the "subject," "author," has been displaced, even in some meaningful sense "killed"; or, that we are undergoing changes in relation to ourselves—as measured by our changing dispositions, attitudes, feelings, and desires about who we are, who others are.

As many claim today, postmodern identity is set adrift, lacking in solidarity, community, structure; according to some tellings, identities can be "tried on" and then "discarded"; or, identities manifest themselves as a refusal to be "tied down" or committed to a single or univocal identity. This idea of our inevitable metamorphoses may be one reason for our relatively recent discovery of and valuing of "transgender." For today, increasing numbers of us more readily accept—extol even—the idea that we might be many things, many selves; flexible selves are increasingly valued (Martin 1994; Turkle 1995, ch. 7). This disposition has long been at the heart of "self-help" products and their proliferation and our efforts to cope with the increasingly competitive and volatile world of today, for example, the instability of work and the loss of work (McGee 2005). This vision of the self in near-endless change and, if we are lucky, "development" is almost too finely tuned to the needs of our present economies and technologies.

As I have also argued here, communication technologies provide some of the newest installments to the narrative of modern identity. To quote from Anthony Elliot (2001, 135), an expert on the topic: "The series of global transitions relating to information technology, computerization and the wholesale commodification of everyday life ... entangles the self in the exhilarating and threatening potentialities of postmodernity as a whole." The metaphors of identity today (which is now "identities") are those of speed, fragmentation, multiplicity, dispersion, and saturation.

Again, the expert speaks: "In a world invaded by new technologies and saturated with flashy commodities, the self loses its consistency, and becomes brittle, broken or shattered ... The flickering media surfaces of postmodern culture are ... mirrored internally" (Elliot 2001, 136).

Today's identity, it is claimed, has lost a sense of itself as something *true* or even *knowable*, due to social and technological "saturation" (Gergen 1991). The bombardment of our senses, the fragmenting and populating of our self-experiences relativizes our sense of what a self is; we are constructions of the moment. This is not entirely newsworthy, but what is new and newsworthy is that more and more people manifest a *consciousness* of this fact. This, in my judgment, may be the most consequential development in the story of postmodern identity—that in the domain of everyday life, the notion has been gaining ground that what we call "culture" is a fact and a force making us different from one another, sometimes in profound and inescapable ways. Alongside this "consciousness of culture" is another consciousness that exists in tension with it—"consciousness of construction" (Gergen's phrase, 1991, 2001)—the idea that the world is something put together which, in its exhilarating version, is the sense that there are "selves" and "identities" to conquer and to claim as our own (McCarthy 1996, 81–4).

While these two features of postmodern identity may appear to be in conflict—that language and culture profoundly shape us and that identity is something variable and something we can fashion—they serve to create the sense that selves today are profoundly variable beings, in thrall to mundane forces, while simultaneously lacking foundations either in the order of being or in nature. This inescapable recognition fosters in us a sense of our "construction": the self and the body have become "sites of interaction," worked on by the techniques and practitioners of postmodernity. Today, neither the body nor one's identity is viewed as a natural object; each is increasingly subject to discursive practices and reflexive action, the kinds provided by

self-help texts and techniques, therapies, exercise machines and man-
uals, plastic surgery, organ transplants. "The body itself ... becomes
more and more immediately relevant to the identity the individual
promotes" (Giddens 1991, 218) or, to an *identity promoted by
a society*.

Michel Foucault's question "What are we today?" contains the
recognition of the "made-up" self, something we produce *ourselves*, as
well as an enlivened sense that our ability to ask the question at all
matters a great deal, in his words the self of today demands a critical
engagement with who we are and who we can imagine ourselves to be:
"a mode of relating to contemporary reality; a voluntary choice made
by certain people; in the end, a way of thinking and feeling; a way too,
of acting and behaving that at one and the same time marks a relation
of belonging and presents itself as a task" (1984. 39).

"What are we today?" The question refers to more than the
activity of philosophizing; it refers to "us," the collective historical
subject of today: "What are we today? What are we in our actuality?"
(Foucault, Martin, Gutman, and Hutton 1988, 145).

IDENTITY AND TODAY'S EMOTIONAL TURN

This returns us (finally) to the topic at hand. Whatever "we" are
appears to be more inscrutable than ever, captured in the elusive
domains of experience and emotion, selves that are also taken apart
(or dispersed) by our own technological inventiveness. (We play at and
pretend to be someone online; we are inventive especially as characters in our own digital productions.) As a number of commentators
have remarked (Gitlin 2002; Gabler 1998; Gergen 1991; Susman 1984),
we can only speak of the shape or contours of identity today, rather
than of *essences* or *entities*: a shape modeled on and responsive to
today's media culture, antinomian in both disposition and action, just
as its preferred mode of action is self-seeking and impulsive. The self
seeks to express and to discover itself in the "environments"—media
images—it consumes, just as it has become skilled in the various
pursuits and pleasures of our consumer culture. But that is not all.

The narrative history of the modern self or identity has taken an emotional turn. While this cultural development has its roots in late eighteenth-century and early nineteenth-century Romanticism, today our feelings and emotions have come to be perceived now—in this Age of Experience—as powerful inner forces of nature and as our deepest and truest and most authentic selves (*Revel Foundry* 2015). Today's postmodern inward-turning self has discovered that its greatest truths and deepest realities are its feelings and emotions. This we have in common with many of our forebears whose stories told of their struggles against the rational ethos of their time to assert the primacy of human feeling and experience (Thompson 1997; Gay 1995).

But this alone does not distinguish our present condition. Rather, it is the *performative or dramatic turn* that is also important as an integral feature of today's emotional lives: our longing to discover and to validate our emotional selves on the many public stages of today's mediatized world. For these stages—however differently we apprehend these events and persons, and, especially, what these different events mean to us—provide us with sites and scripts to know and to become the emotional players we long to be: at the memorials and funerals we attend for city cops killed on our streets or at those services we attend for the black victims killed by cops; the disasters that fill up our minds, minds that overflow with the images of human suffering near and far; the over-scripted concerts and sports events we attend (on screen or in person) as fans whose emotions compete for center stage with the players and performers we came to watch. Somehow our mediatized world holds out to us promises of feeling and being, promises that we attach to these public stages and events.

In our time, the enormous appeal of drama and performance found expression, among academics, in the work of Erving Goffman, who gave us an image of ourselves as actors always and inescapably engaged in roles and in the "presentation of self in everyday life." These works came to us at a time—the late 1950s and early 1960s—when Americans had not yet become conscious of our own theatricality. In fact, this was a time before "entertainment conquered reality," to steal Neal Gabler's phrase (1998), which means when everything in America from politics and religion to sex and consumption had been touched by the brush of showbiz and the culture of celebrity. *The Presentation of Self in Everyday Life* not only brought something new into sociology but also entered our world when we were on the brink of discovering the singular role of *performance* in our culture, a time when drama and acting would become part of our everyday lives, drama as habitual experience, as Raymond Williams has called it ([1974] 1989, 3–5).

Goffman's analogy of the stage was important for understanding the impact of both his work and his vision of social life. Even though others used drama and performance to study human relationships and social rituals (Burke 1945, 1973; V. Turner 1988), Goffman took the analogy of the theater very far indeed with his elaborations of impression management and the back- and front-stage regions of performances and his claim that we play roles in and out of character, that "one's face is a sacred thing" (1967, 19), a thing requiring ritual to sustain it. He also argued that emotions correspond to various ritual moves and ritual stages and that these rituals presume a great deal of perceptiveness and social skill, similar to the skills of professional actors (1959, 254–5). Goffman also claimed that the "proper study of interaction" (1967, 2), his playful inversion of Alexander Pope's famous phrase, is really about the formal relations among actors themselves—the lines they draw, the roles they insist on, the signs they exchange, the distances between them, what they make of each other—and "not the individual and his psychology" (2). The proper study of interaction is not the individuals who make up this or that transactional moment, "but rather the syntactical relations among the acts of different persons mutually present to one another" (2).

Goffman's dramaturgy, along with the growing consciousness of drama in our everyday lives (R. Williams [1974] 1989, 3–5), contributed, I think, to some of the changing meanings of "public life" in postmodern culture. At some point in our recent history, what we call public life ceased to be known by us as the place where inauthentic roles were performed out of obligation or necessity, whether the workplace or the office cocktail party or the encounter with the many strangers that made up our "society." Public life, however many conflicting meanings and messages it brought to mind, was becoming a world of performances, a place of happenings, a place "where the action was," where risk and danger brought the promise of fun and some real emotion (Goffman 1967).

The emotional turn of a mediatized world—postmodernity—holds out to us appealing and pleasurable public places and digitized sites and new communities. It also holds out to us entire worlds, like Disney World or Six Flags Adventure and Safari, opportunities for all forms of tourism; these have allowed us to play, like actors do, at "identities," to try on our imagined selves and to see how they fit and feel as we stroll as spectator-performers at shopping malls or urban parks and playgrounds or as fans entertained at TV studios, as tourists on a luxury cruise ship, online before the cruise begins or on the cruise ship itself. Sites—brick and mortar or digital—like these offer us worlds of play and fantasy (Ritzer 2004), places where we can try on identities for fun and games. But these performances are, in effect, so many dress rehearsals for the more serious and far darker dramas we seek out in the form of highly mediatized funerals, rituals at sites of disaster, monuments to our dead soldiers or to victims of global terror (A. Kleinman and J. Kleinman 1997). May we even speak of the *appeal* of these sites of death and disaster? My answer is, yes, we can, because of the deeply felt emotions they hold out to us. Emotion and feeling are the ways we come in contact with ourselves as we really are or want to be, selves who feel things deeply. Authentic selves.

We have come to learn and to trust many public sites as places where reality is played out in the *real emotions* we feel. Those sites, then, include the full range of places, from those where we seek out fun and pleasure in everyday life to those others where we can remember the many tragedies and sufferings we encounter "firsthand" in our mediatized world.

There may be a truth in the assertion that "we are all actors."
But today we have become spectator-actors, participants in dramas we
seek out on the many stages that offer us the emotions we yearn to
feel, dramas of self that we attend as spectators and performers.
The "realities" we speak of today are the very feelings and emotions
we encounter on these stages and in these performances. In what
follows, I take up this argument in greater detail by examining the
growing popularity of monuments and memorials to death and disaster, trying to understand what these emotional sites mean for the
many of us who travel to these sites to remember events that we
never witnessed firsthand.

3 Emotional Sites of Death and Destruction

It is now commonplace to take notice of the popularity of
memorialization in American culture ... With the Vietnam Veterans
Memorial as a model, individuals did not hesitate to shape the meaning of
a memorial through their own actions and energies.

Edward T. Linenthal (2001, 133–4)

The American way of death ... seems to be tending toward desire these
days. The instantaneous monuments that are tossed together with
flowers, stuffed animals, and personal messages ... suggest that the
country is ready, even eager, to connect with death and the past, no matter
how superficial that connection may sometimes be.

Roger Rosenblatt (2000, 28)

Most of us will be remembering an event we never saw, which is precisely
the character of collective memory.

Leon Wieseltier (2002, 38)

The first thing to say about it [the National September 11 Memorial and
Museum], and maybe the last, is that it's emotionally overwhelming ...

Holland Carter (2014)

PRELIMINARIES

One of the very first signs to me that emotions had taken on a new
form—surprising me in the ways that the change announced itself and
by what it said about honoring the dead—were the new and very
public displays of grief and mourning that began to appear on my
own city streets and in my neighborhood as well as on the nightly
news in recent decades. These shrines to mark the deaths of both
strangers and friends, very public figures as well as those close to us,
began to appear everywhere in the late 1970s, although one of the first
expressions of this kind took place in Dallas, Texas, after the assassination of President John F. Kennedy in November 1962. In the after-
math of the assassination, mounds of flowers, candles, wreaths, and
mementos were left at the site of the killing. This site also became one

71

of the first memorial museums in the United States. The Sixth Floor Museum at Dealey Plaza contains a permanent historical exhibition whose focus is on the impact of Kennedy's death on the nation and the world.

There have been many other public displays for those who, like Kennedy, few knew personally but many mourned. In some of these cases, early examples that are now more commonplace, instant shrines were assembled within hours of the events: outside the New York City apartment house of John Lennon in 1980; in Union, South Carolina, where Susan Smith drowned her two young children in 1994; at Sixth Street and Hudson, a few blocks from the site of the 1995 Oklahoma City bombing; on the beach near the spot off Fire Island where 230 passengers of TWA Flight 800 died in 1996; at Kensington Palace in London in the days following the deadly car crash of Diana, Princess of Wales, in 1997; at Columbine High School for the fifteen young people killed during the violent rampage there on April 20, 1999. For many, these displays of mourners and the gifts they laid for the fallen signaled something new about death and dying. Of course not entirely new, for people have always mourned their dead, but new in the public nature of the grieving and new in the sense that the fallen were not known personally by those who mourned them so extravagantly.

In this chapter, I examine these displays of grief and mourning as *cultural practices*. So construed, culture is something—many things, really—observable and material; culture is done, as much as it is thought and felt (see chapter 1). But my principal focus is on the issue of *emotional cultures* today and, to that end, I am using these displays of grief and mourning as resources for identifying today's emotional cultures. For what we social scientists call "emotional cultures" are embedded, as it were, in these practices, as are moral self-understandings, notions of self and identity: that is, who I *really* am (whatever that "really" refers to), *how* the self is construed, *what* it believes itself to be, *how* it is connected (or not connected) to other selves, whether or not it believes in its own individuality. These aspects of identity, what Raymond Williams has called a people's "structure of sentiment," are closely related to what I mean here by emotional culture, and these are, in the final analysis, what I am looking for.

MUSEUMS, MONUMENTS, AND MEMORIALS

The topic of study, *contemporary forms of memorializing*, is one that is typically examined together with the related subjects of museums and monuments; all three—memorials, museums, monuments—are framed as part of *collective identity*, such as national identity, the personal and cultural feeling of belonging to a nation, a people, and *collective memory*, how a people knows itself and constructs that knowledge of itself out of its present and its past. In modern societies, in particular, a people's memory and its identity are shaped by public and official "sites of memory" (Huyssen 1995, 250): the *museum* represents how collecting and display are crucial processes of Western identity formation, for example, embodying hierarchies of value, exclusions, and so forth; "identity" here being a kind of wealth of objects, knowledges, memories, and experiences (Clifford 1988, 218; see also Anderson [1983] 1991, ch. 10). The *monument*, such as the tombstone or cross, refers to objects and sculptures used to memorialize persons or events; *memorials*, both mournful and celebratory, are memory-sites as well as designated days, times, and assemblies. Monuments and memorials can serve similar functions, but monuments are a subset of memorials.

In the contemporary study of monument-museum-memorial, initiated by Huyssen (1995), many have observed that recent changes have brought about a merging of these three institutional forms; boundaries have become fluid and there is a new "hybrid memorial media culture" (255) and a popular reclaiming of these forms in urban centers and other public places. Today, the question "What is an art gallery?" is being raised by those who question the function of the gallery or museum as a place of display of finished art works, replacing it with an idea more fluid: art itself as something in process and

revision, something "performed" (Smith 2006; Coulter-Smith 2006).
"Museums are morphing," Edward Rothstein (2006) writes:

> Once they were chroniclers or collectors, gathering objects and facts
> and putting them on display. Now many have become crucibles:
> places where a cultural identity is hammered out, refined and
> reshaped. Along the way they also have become community
> centers, where a group gathers to celebrate its past, commemorate
> its tragedies and convey its achievements to others.

Related to these recent changes is another change, namely, that
the expansion of mass media and consumer culture has acted as a force
in these transformations. Today, for example, museums have become
marketplaces for the consumption of goods as they are places for art
shows and extravaganzas and places of mass education and entertainment: the commercialized museum moving closer to the world of
spectacle, becoming a "bazaar" that dispenses its very own "spiritual
products." Similarly, objects that museums display and sell have been
subject to "commodification," whether art products themselves,
souvenirs of value, or objects of everyday life (tote bags, T-shirts,
mugs, umbrellas) dispensed by museum shops (Debeljak 1998; Kaya
and Yağiz 2015).

The growth and expansion of these institutions, as well as the
surge of academic and scholarly interest in the museum, monument,
and memorial, can be seen as marks of their importance, an importance with simultaneous links to changes in today's markets as much
as to changes in the mass media that simultaneously drive markets
and cultural forms, from advertising and entertainment to religion and
politics.

Memorializing today has even been described as possessing an
"intensity" (Huyssen 1995, 253), pointing to the range of engagements
with the process (scholarly, popular, journalistic, political) and to the
extraordinary rise in memorials and in new forms of memorializing.
Take for example, the sheer proliferation of memorials and their
popularity: Holocaust memorials and museums are now numbered

in the thousands worldwide and visitors to these memorials are now estimated in the millions (Young 1993, x). In Washington, DC, we have witnessed the most active period of building monuments in a century; for the Washington Mall alone, this includes the Vietnam Veterans Memorial, the Korean War Veterans Memorial, the Franklin Delano Roosevelt Memorial, and the National World War II Memorial. In fact, in 2000, US government planners unveiled 102 possible sites for this century's new memorials and museums in Washington. In the first two decades since its building in 1982, the Vietnam Veterans Memorial—by far, the most popular memorial in the country—has been visited by at least fifty million people and has consistently drawn large numbers of visitors; despite the fact that "there is no liturgical calendar of rites there, nor is there a prescribed routine or custom that the acts of remembrance must follow; but the commemoration is regular, and everyday people go there to remember" (Butterfield 2003, 32; cf. Lin 2000).

More recent estimates report monthly visitors to the Vietnam Veterans Memorial in the hundreds of thousands (Janiskee 2010) and in 2012 the reported estimate for one year was 4.2 million (Greenspan 2012). The Oklahoma City National Memorial, dedicated in April 2000, received 340,000 visitors in its first five months alone (Linenthal 2001, 231); in its first nine years, more than 4.4 million visitors have toured the historic site (Oklahoma City National Memorial 2016).

The Vietnam Veterans Memorial, opened in 1982, and the Oklahoma City National Memorial, in 2001, mark important changes in the culture of modern or postmodern memorials. Scholars describe a "memorial impulse" today (Butterfield 2003, 28), an "expansive historicism" of our culture (Huyssen 1995, 254), one claiming that "never before has a cultural present been obsessed with the past" as we had been in the 1970s and 1980s (Hermann Lübbe as cited in Huyssen 1995, 253). These claims are noteworthy against a background where the very notion of a modern monument was seen as a contradiction in terms.

The "death" of the monument and the museum has been proclaimed many times: "monumental" was Nietzsche's "disdainful epithet" for any version of history calling itself permanent (Young 1993, 4). Lewis Mumford's *The Culture of Cities* (1938) argued that monuments had lost their aesthetic and social legitimacy. This academic or scholarly view, that "memory is an impediment to modernity" (Butterfield 2003, 27), its progressive impulse, has been widely shared by architects, city planners, and artists and was especially pronounced by the 1960s with its antinomian ethos, its skepticism about common values, its abhorrence of war, along with the view that monuments speak only of state power; *monuments are principally ideological*, marking a nation's history by its soldiers' deaths, meaningful only in nationalist and patriotic terms. Accordingly, monuments have been said to "bury memory" (an argument of the late German historian Martin Broszat, see Young 1999) just as they absorb and displace memory. In fact, monuments and memorials can be said to aid in the process of forgetting things and events of horrific proportion. I only very quickly touched upon some of the terms of these debates in order to raise my own concerns relative to changing emotional cultures: this body of critical opinion about monuments and memorials, which dominated public and academic discourse through the 1960s and 1970s, suggests that today's engagement with memorializing is of interest and importance as both recent cultural history and emotional history.

Both the Vietnam Veterans Memorial and the Oklahoma City National Memorial have been said to represent new memorial forms in the United States, as well as changing public sensibilities about memorializing; some even view these memorials as forces in themselves, changing the opinion of many that the memorial was dead. These memorials—the one, to the 58,000 dead and missing American soldiers of the Vietnam War; the second, the memorial for the 168 people killed at the federal building in Oklahoma City—represent an iconography described as both highly emotional and individualist, appealing directly and emotionally to individuals and not to any cause or collectivity (Lin 2000). While there have been many readings and interpretations of these public memorials, descriptions like the following are typical.

Maya Ying Lin, the designer of the Vietnam Veterans Memorial stated that her design was not meant to communicate a political message but to evoke "feelings, thoughts, and emotions" of an individual or private nature (as cited in Wagner-Pacifici and Schwartz 1991, 393; see also Lin 1996): "What people see or don't see is their own projection," she wrote (Lin 1996, 524). From Paul Golberger's (2004a) opening statement, in his review of US war memorials: "few war memorials evoke deep, gut-wrenching emotion. Maya Lin's astonishingly simple Vietnam Veterans Memorial does." Further, Goldberger has commented (2009, 205; see also 2004b; Lin, Brenson, Fox, Goldberger 2015) on the significance of the 58,000 names engraved on Lin's stone wall and the importance of the relationship between the wall and the landscape: "We descend, then rise again, as if to return to the land of the living—[which] is deeply moving." Similarly, the 168 bronze and glass chairs, clustered on a grassy slope and etched with the name of each person, honoring the 168 dead at Oklahoma City, constitute the main component of the memorial; they are positioned in nine rows that correspond to floors of the building where each of the victims were when the bomb exploded (Linenthal 2001).

The architectural term applied to both these memorials and to others is "minimalist," the unofficial language of modernist art since mid-century, but only recently used for monuments and memorials: Lin's Vietnam Veterans Memorial, Peter Eisenman's Holocaust Memorial in Berlin (a field of plain concrete pillars like headstones), Oklahoma City's grid of chairs. These memorials are not only important signifiers of the individual lives lost, they commemorate ordinary people, not something that memorials have done until relatively recently. In fact, as highly individualized cultural forms, they represent a type of "anti-memorial" (Kimmelman 2002; Ware 2008), something sentimental and populist. In one critic's words, this is an art form with an "emotional intensity" and one that allows, even welcomes, the popular and emotional and individual gestures of its visitors: at the Vietnam Veterans Memorial people go to read, touch the names, leave flowers and photos—"mementos are one of the great mysteries of the Wall" (Ayres 1992). Kimmelman (2002) calls "the modern memorial sublime," a grandeur that has nothing to do with the heroic monument, the generalized image of a uniformed soldier holding a gun or flag. And while its form allows for the evocation of lives of individuals—their beings, voices—the minimalist memorial is mute.

This is one feature of the Vietnam Veterans Memorial that caused so much of the controversy surrounding it: on the original design, the word "Vietnam" did not even appear. This is one feature of what is called "minimalism," its ideological silence; its appeal to many, including the judges that selected it, was what it did *not* say; it made death in war a private matter, rather than a sacrifice for a collective cause. Yet, the memorial's strong appeal and resonance was also its ability to capture our collective feelings of ambiguity and anguish about the Vietnam War and our agreement that those who died should be remembered (Wagner-Pacifici and Schwartz 1991, 395).

I'd like to insert here one of my study's concerns, its relationship to the modern history of emotions. Twentieth-century public reserve surrounding grief and memorializing has been well-documented (e.g., P. Stearns 2007; Bryant 2003; Lofland 1985). That is, for most of the twentieth century and even today among some groups, regions, and classes in the United States, intense and public grief and mourning are, in important ways, socially unacceptable. (I speak of the duration and the quality of our display of grief.) That is, if we compare ourselves to our Victorian predecessors, who mourned extravagantly. Clearly, the emotions surrounding public memorializing open new questions as to the rise of these memorials, their popularity, and the need or disposition for expressions of public mourning and memorial sites.

Both the Vietnam and Oklahoma City memorials—in their minimalist muteness—allow for (invite, really) an abundance of individual and popular expressions at the sites, expressions like those at local and instant sites of loss and mourning on highways and on neighborhood streets. At the Vietnam Veterans Memorial visitors have left so many things—flowers, photos, letters, medals, even a Harley-Davidson motorcycle—that there is an entire warehouse to preserve them. Individual names, often traced by visitors, are also personally and emotionally significant; the names are touched lovingly, "caressed" really (Wagner-Pacifici and Schwartz 1991, 403). Maya Lin (2000) has told of her first visit to the completed memorial, when she, like those mourners she imagined while designing this memorial, went to look for and touched the name of a friend's father.

For some, the emotional and personal responses of visitors—the aggrieved—are a spectacle "more moving than the Memorial Wall itself" (Wagner-Pacifici and Schwartz 1991, 403). Yet the wall itself, its polished marble reflecting us back to ourselves, can also be seen as an evoker of personal sentiments; the names functioning as the objects of a highly individualized, yet collective, ritual (Wagner-Pacifici and Schwartz 1991, 404). The chairs at Oklahoma City are like these names: "The bronze back and frames of the chairs them-selves were dipped individually, to remind [us] that these were people. No two chairs are alike" (Rosenblatt 2000, 28). At the Holocaust museum in Washington, two particularly emotionally wrenching objects on view are the empty shoes of the dead and the hall of photo-graphs of those who were killed in the camps. But there is also the identification card the visitor is handed on entering the exhibit; "this card tells the story of a real person who lived during the Holocaust," a person carried with the visitor through the exhibit.

Besides invoking the lives of individual persons, today's memor-ials are *democratic*; not only celebrating ordinary people but also "created in the name of and for the uses of ordinary people ... [offering us] places where ordinary people can reach a personal understanding" (Rosenblatt 2000, 29). And today's moveable and Internet memorials are "*more fluid, less set in stone*," as are those replications of memor-ials in numbers of US towns and cities. In one of my city neighborhoods where I still return, called Inwood, in upper Manhattan, for example, a large steel crossbeam, from New York City's "ground zero," stands next to a Catholic church, surrounded by the individual markers (with names and photos) of firefighters and other first-responders who died on 9/11, members of this parish church. This space is kept as a sacred space and is now regarded as part of the churchyard itself; a gate allows visitors to stop and honor the dead who are remembered in this space, a space located right next to the church building but also the city sidewalk on Isham Street near Broadway.

Museums and memorials today are also designed to be *experiential*, transforming those who visit them. Edward Linenthal, author of books on the Holocaust and Oklahoma City memorials, has said that they are designed so that "the memory of the event will be as transforming as the event itself" (an interview cited in Rosenblatt 2000, 29). Many of them, and this is certainly the case for Washington's Holocaust museum, are *teaching institutions*, telling a story of the event using film, photo, and video; the new National World War II Memorial includes a teaching museum. These are places of "civic transformation"; one is expected to come away changed, and there are many testimonies of this occurring for those who visit these memorials. Linenthal has described another function of these memorials: they are sites where we discover meanings as well as aspects of our identities. In his words, "Memorials are a product of who we are right now. We are a people negotiating our identities ... In part, we are doing this by creating and feeling the power of memorials" (cited in Rosenblatt 2000, 30).

I want to insert here a statement about my cultural method of studying memorials. It is, of course, highly selective as a way to access today's emotions and their place in our structure of feeling. For, in our postmodern lives, we may access multiple sources in order to study the many different ways that we record and interpret, remember and forget the human horrors and atrocities that we have come to know *as our own*. Works of fiction can also be used, like memorials, to examine today's structure of feeling. Consider, for example, W. G. Sebald's evocations of the Holocaust and the European destruction of World War II in his novels—events so catastrophic that paradoxically they seem (perhaps lost to us) buried by history and memory. In his last novel *Austerlitz* (2001), we accompany the wanderings of Jacques Austerlitz as he tries to recover a life lost to him by memory and physical displacement when he was brought to England as an infant in 1939 as part of an attempt to save the children of European Jewry (the so-called *Kindertransporte*). Searching for his past through what is no longer there, and yet is—a lost European civilization—Austerlitz comes at one point to Theresienstadt (where his mother may have been sent), the Nazi "model" ghetto/concentration camp, now a museum/memorial. There, surrounded by the museum's artifacts, Austerlitz experiences a brief intense representation of the actual life of the camp. Sebald has called his novels "documentary fictions."

Sebald's writings (for a commentary, see O'Connell 2011) also help us to understand the problem we confront today when we try to write about the horrible events of the last century. For the most important events of our time were, in many cases, too terrible to remember and to record. So we—writers, social scientists, historians— go to objects and buildings, to things and to places that can speak to us of events in our past, events that assist us in the work of uncovering memory (Laqueur [1980] 1988).

In this sense, today's memorials and museums to death and war are *more than memorials*, they are designed and built to remember, to uncover memory, but for other purposes too: they are redemptive, educational, and therapeutic, designed for us today so we can project on their walls and into their objects our own feelings, as the architect Maya Lin invited us to do (Lin, as cited in Wagner-Pacifici and Schwartz 1991; see also Lin 1996, 2000). The postmodern memorial is also part of today's ever-expanding media environment, not only shaped by its technologies but responsive to our highly reflexive and audience-based perspectives. For a memorial to be built, there needs to be a publicly felt need and desire "to enter into the event," and this requires that it be framed by the media in that way (Glazer 1996).

A memorial provides an occasion to enter and to experience and to remember an event, a place, a person's life—things that are, for many of us, remote, but nonetheless experienced as real. Most of us are "remembering" events that we never witnessed directly (Wieseltier 2002). Yet in some important sense, they seem to us to have been experienced *as our own*. Today, because of mass media, we also have deep attachments to people we never met and whom we don't know in any immediate sense (Calhoun 1991a). This is also true of events that we witness again and again; we feel the need to personally acknowledge, ritually and publicly, the death of someone we never knew, or a collective horrific act that happened before our eyes on a screen, in living color. We believe we live in reality, but in fact we live, in part, in the world of the *imaginary real*. For these reasons and others, the project I have been describing—a cultural study about emotions and emotional cultures today—has taken a turn toward mass media as one of the forces changing both the *sites* of collective emotional practices—memorials, museums, sports arenas—as well as the *actions and experiences* of people themselves.

Equally important, it seems to me, is the topic of *identity* (addressed in chapter 2). Clearly, we are witnessing in our time yet another change in the character of the modern self—a change that will further enlighten us about the emotional practices I have described here. In fact, to state the case in the strongest terms: *these emotional practices, these public emotional dramas require not only a particular setting conducive to displays of strong feelings; they also require a certain kind of social actor, one disposed to participate in and to enact feelings associated with memories of death, separation, and sadness.* But why our public dramas have become so *emotional* is the principal question I have raised here. The postmodern memorial points to a few of the answers. To highlight some of them:

These new memorial sites are consequential for what we feel and how we experience our emotions at these sites, for they situate and frame the emotional acts themselves. The sites are designed and arranged as settings for the democratic masses who visit them, directing our movements—down a grassy slope at the Vietnam Veterans Memorial to read the wall of 58,195 names, inside a steel elevator like those in the death camps at the Holocaust museum, into hallways displaying life-sized photos of victims, into small movie theaters to watch films of disastrous events or to watch and listen to the stories of those who witnessed them directly. Not only do museums and memorials like these function as settings or public stages on which to assemble, to remember, to mourn, or to undergo a cultural education about "our times," but in doing these things, they also point to something new on our social landscape: they operate as new moral spaces that borrow heavily from the now-familiar world of media—photos, films, TV, and recorded sound. At the National September 11 Memorial and Museum in New York, for example, the numerous exhibits feature audio- and videotapes and recorded testimonies of 9/11/2001.

This memorial-museum (one of the new hybrids) is extraordinary in many of the ways discussed here, including for its sheer size; the exhibition itself, at the 9/11 memorial and museum, occupies 110,000 square feet at the heart of the World Trade Center site (see Carter 2014; Goldberger 2004b); one can also tour the site itself at the Ground Zero & 9/11 Memorial Tour; tours include the Freedom Tower Observatory.

Like this broader media culture we inhabit in our everyday lives, we attend these sites as *media events*; we gather there as *spectator-participants* seeking meaningful experiences, whether memorializing the victims of the Holocaust or of the bombing of the federal building in Oklahoma City or the attack at New York's World Trade Center. As the *New York Times* art critic, Holland Carter, wrote on the media features of the 9/11 memorial and museum: "the experience of moving through this museum is at once theatrical, voyeuristic and devotional" (Carter 2014).

These new public sites—symbols themselves—also draw us to themselves to remember something we "witnessed." *They also represent new "arenas of action" that combine public and private itudes, feelings, and dispositions.* These sites "beckon new types of social performances ... new collective configurations" (Cerulo 1997, 397). Public assemblies at these sites neither draw from nor strengthen common sentiments and beliefs. Yet, they are remarkably intense, enveloping spectators in experiences of something important, not in a strictly political but in a deeply personal sense about something that "really happened" to each of us.

Acts of Emotional Identification

Some of the emotional cultural practices described here are closely linked to processes of "identification," a concept borrowed from both cultural studies and psychoanalysis. Identification—attachments and belongings—is constructed around *commonalities* imagined, felt, recognized, asserted, or imposed. Identification engages ideas and images about one's own or a group's solidarity and allegiance—its loss, its achievement—yet never one of these, as "identification" in modern dress is fraught with indeterminacy; identification points to a desire for, indeed, *a fantasy of incorporation* (Hall 1996, 3). Identification suggests that some of these collective happenings—gatherings like demonstrations in public spaces, but also some entertainment events like rock concerts—are dramas of finding and losing: of group memory, of lost youth and the emotional intensity these memories and identities evoke. I am thinking right now of the fans of Bruce Springsteen reminiscing about the fortieth anniversary (September 13, 2015) of one of the greatest rock-and-roll albums ever made, "Born to Run" of 1975 (Hickey 2015). Or, check out the fans' nostalgic and emotional postings about the "Piano Man" himself, Billy Joel, on billyjoelfan.com.

Yet, for us postmoderns, *identification can be either "too much" or "too little,"* at least for a sizable number of us (Hall 1996, 2–3). For it conjures up the modern and postmodern fear of being engulfed by others, while lonely in our autonomy, experiences narrated by Freud, Marx, and Durkheim. For we have no bonds that are unbreakable, no final attachments, we are desperate to relate, yet wary of the state of "being related," as Zygmunt Bauman writes about our "liquidity" (2005, viii).

Like all signifying practices, identifications are both "strategic" and "positional"; they entail "discursive work, the binding and making of symbolic boundaries" (Hall 1996, 3). So conceived, identities today are "points of temporary attachment" (Holstein and Gubrium 2000), ephemeral and fleeting like emotions themselves and, like some popular and local roadside shrines assembled to commemorate a loss intensely felt, they can be quickly abandoned, even the large shrines of flowers and remembrances assembled to honor the two NYC cops killed on December 20, 2014, Wenjian Liu and Rafael Ramos; the shrine was removed only weeks later.

A theory of identification can also be used to explore the new identities and attachments produced by mass media, those deeply felt (but fleeting) attachments to people we never met and whom we do not know in any immediate sense (Calhoun 1991a; Meyrowitz 1985; on "belonging" see Calhoun 2013). Identification can assist us in understanding the many new forums that publics seek out to express their sympathy and grief: sites of airplane crashes, house burnings, or schools where children died (Fernandez 2007a, 2007b; Fernandez and Williams 2007).

Another concept useful for the interpretation of these materials is that of Reddy's (2001) theory of "emotives." Emotives are emotional expressions that describe the process by which emotions are thought about, managed, and shaped by social actors as they seek to express how and what they feel in the terms of the culture they share and produce. Emotives are instruments for directly changing, building, hiding, and intensifying emotions (Reddy 2001, 105), operating on our emotions in unexpected ways. For, only as people articulate their feelings can they "know" what they feel, reflect on this knowledge, and feel yet more (Rosenwein 2002).

The idea of emotives points to a kind of freedom of persons to *navigate* (Reddy's term) the culture and styles of emotion imposed by a society and by hierarchies of class and literacy. Emotional expressions, then, do more than shape what we feel to conform to perceived norms; emotives are also *self-altering capacities*—what we can *say* about what we feel, what we *think* about our feelings—for these sayings and these thoughts enable us to navigate in the complex cultural worlds we inhabit.

We are now in a better position to ask questions and find possible answers about the significance of the public displays of emotion. One obvious interpretive avenue is that of people's *expressive capacities* relative to the cultures they are navigating. In my studies, I pose the question: *What do people themselves make of the feelings they are having and pursuing as spectator-participants in the growing number of public stages and forums for collective action and emotion?* When this is asked, many of those who grieve and mourn admit an inability to understand their own feelings when public figures die: "feeling like a member of my family has passed away," one man said to me. A woman, speaking to a *New York Times* reporter said that "she found she was feeling sadder about the Kennedy plane crash [of John F. Kennedy Jr. on July 16, 1999] than she did about the fatal car crash of her sister back in 1949 (C. Goldberg 1999). Visitors to the Vietnam shrine told me that they came *to feel something* (they needed to come here to feel their grief, to feel solace), to bring "closure" to the death of a friend or loved one. One woman told a reporter that she found more solace at the site of a local war memorial after her brother's death in Iraq than she found at his funeral and burial ceremony.[1]

The idea of emotives returns us to the centerpiece of the psychoanalytic project—personal life itself—and to the idea that cultures, no matter how powerful, exist relative to something personal, inchoate, imaginary, emotional, and experiential (Zaretsky 2004). In fact, Freudian analysis requires—in the face of our emotions and conflicts—that we give articulation to our "inner depths"; it is precisely in that articulation that we can regain our freedom and our self-possession, ideas compatible with the theory of emotives.

Conclusion

I think that there is something very important about the dramatic and public settings of the memorials I describe here and to the *mediated* quality of these and other collective actions and social performances: our participation at these events and our attendance at these shrines take place both on the screens we watch and in our face-to-face "real life" participation with others who are gathered there. The events we view on screens are framed for us and offer us others' emotional gestures of grief and mourning; they can also—as media events— serve as sites of a group's public statement and as occasions for organized political protest (Greenberg 2015).

These mediated settings of public actions also suggest a new form of "agency"—a self-conscious, collective agency whereby social actors (when you ask them) attest to a conscious sense of the moral good of acting with others to pursue and to secure that good (victims' families seeking to authorize a public memorial, bereaved widows of fallen soldiers, mothers against drunk driving, mourners in processions of firefighters). When media effectively sever the connection between ourselves and physical places (Meyrowitz 1985), new social spaces, new arenas of action arise, as do "new types of social performances" (Cerulo 1997, 397), and new identities and identifications. Technologies of communication provide not only a "torrent" of images and sensations but also conditions for our knowledge of distant and unknown things, previously unimagined objects and others that effectively "saturate our way of life with a promise of feeling" (Gitlin 2002, 6; cf. Altheide and Snow 1979, 41–55).

Jeffrey Alexander and his colleagues (2006) describe such social performances as dramas of "authenticity," referring to the growing number of intense and emotional social performances today and to the fact that increasingly dramas are built into the rhythms of our every- day lives, where social actors across a range of public venues impli- citly orient themselves and their actions on a public stage, "seeking identification with their experiences and understandings from their

Social performance

audiences" (Alexander and Mast 2006, 2). Authenticity, then, the idea and ideal of "being real" to ourselves and to others, becomes part of today's dramas of self and deeply felt emotion. Put differently, dramas become so many vehicles holding out to us promises of real emotion, authentic emotion, authentic selfhood. As we have stated earlier (preface), Raymond Williams alerted us to this possibility, pointing out that as a society, we have never "acted so much or watched so many others acting ... What we have now is drama as habitual experience" (R. Williams [1974] 1989, 3–5).

Charles Taylor's (2004, 2007) concept of the "social imaginary"— the deep "normative notions and images that underlie these expectations"—offers an even broader and more dense account of the cultural and personal schemes that these social dramas signify. Since the nineteenth century, he argues (drawing from the work of Benedict Anderson on national identity), a new way of construing "society" develops, a collectivity of "individuals" existing simultaneously, persons whose lives occur in (secular) time: "society" ("We the people ... ") existing horizontally, developing and changing through sequences of events. In today's "direct-access society," each of us is "immediate to the whole" (2004, 158). The rise of various postmodern social forms and movements draws from this revolution in our social imaginary; today the images of "direct access" are increasingly socially diffused (2004, 159–60):

> People conceive themselves as participating directly in
> a nationwide (sometimes even international) discussion . . . .
> We see ourselves in spaces of fashion ... taking up and handing on styles; we see ourselves as part of the worldwide audience of media stars. And though these spaces are in their own sense hierarchical —they center on quasi-legendary figures—they offer all
> participants an access unmediated by any of their other allegiances or belongings.

These modes of "imagined direct access" are "egalitarian" as more of us—unlike our forebears—are relatively free from the mediation of authorities or, more importantly, we *experience ourselves that way.* We imagine ourselves as both part of and participants in vast communities of nation, social movements, humankind. Society itself has become construed as a "field of common agency." This postmodern social imaginary expands the repertory of our collective actions and creates new social spaces to act on and within *as our own*: urban centers and parks, theaters and museums, mass gatherings to hear political candidates, funerals of celebrities, but even places like television studios, where fans and onlookers show up in increasing numbers. These sites—identity sites—hold out an "immense appeal" (157–61), for they are sites that contain, in some cases, the promise of shared emotion and, in others, the sense of participating in something that is happening *now*—"It's so 'now'!" The television news version is "Breaking News," an announcement that runs along the bottom of our TV screens and flashes to us its important and pressing message, offering us the excitement of being in on some good or terrible event as it happens now.

When people describe themselves to reporters covering some recent death or disaster or act of violence, they often express what they are feeling (whether prompted to do so by the reporter or not): that something deeply emotional and something "real" is happening to them in these public settings of grief. In this way, it might be said, that visitors to a street memorial become part of the spectacle they attend, while sensing that they now belong to a bereaved community (Linenthal 2001, 2–3). So, on the CNN television channel (December 13, 2015), the journalist Poppy Harlow reported on those people in San Bernardino who were going to the street-side shrine erected to honor the fourteen dead after the December 2 mass killings there. A woman interviewed on the news show said to Poppy: "All day, families, friends, and community people have come to honor the victims ... Families need to come here to grieve and to process this tragic event."

Collective acts like these meet a felt or expressed need for many to "process" terrible events, mediatized events like these (A. Kleinman and J. Kleinman 1997). These acts also seek to overcome—to "eclipse"—distance and separation between subject and object, to overcome the separation of the viewer and the object experienced.[2]

4   Mass Emotions in an Age of Mass Media

> The novel and the newspaper ... provided the technical means for "representing" the kind of imagined community that is the nation.
>
> Benedict Anderson ([1983] 1991, 25)

> The building of imagined communities is dramatically accelerated by broadcast media and applies well beyond the range of religions and nationalisms.
>
> Craig Calhoun (1991a, 110)

> The use of communication media involves the creation of new forms of action and interaction ... new kinds of social relationship and new ways of relating to others and oneself.
>
> John B. Thompson (1995, 4)

The distinctive and changing types of social relationships in modern societies are a central topic of works identified with "modernity" itself, sociological texts written from the eighteenth century through the early twentieth century, from Montesquieu and Karl Marx to Max Weber, Emile Durkheim, and Georg Simmel. These texts contain varied accounts of how the new societies of this period (discussed in chapter 2), in Europe and North America, underwent changes in the ways that people were connected to one another, to groups, and to their communities (e.g., Durkheim's types of "social solidarity") and how various types of social groups and communities were integrated, how they were held together as "industrial" or "capitalist" or "democratic" societies.

As we now understand and interpret these texts, they contain narratives, assertions of fact and argument, some clearly "ideological," parochial, or prejudicial for today's readers, a contentious collection of systematic views on industrial society, on capitalist labor and class relations, on the new forms of democracy and "equality of condition," views difficult to compare and even more difficult to reconcile. Despite these difficulties, the theme of changing types of social relationships was always addressed in one form or another by these writers.

The problem I wish to address here concerns the new forms of group activities, or "cultural practices," today, particularly those public displays of emotionality (chapter 1) that have quickly become part of contemporary life not only in the United States and Europe but, in some instances, globally as well: the rise of global sports entertainment spectacles, the emotional intensity of popular concerts by rock groups and singers like Billy Joel and Bruce Springsteen, the rise of new public forums to mark death and disaster (chapter 3). I have already argued (McCarthy 2009) that virtually all of these new forms of public and emotional display are both disseminated and consumed through new forms of mass media (cable television, twenty-four-hour news networks, the Internet) and new technologies (cell phones that transmit sound and video and operate as cameras and keep us wired to the Internet). In other words, the intensity of daily life, its pace and its speed as experienced by social actors today, is one that comes to us through the new forms of media that keep us receiving news and information, keep us entertained or entertaining each other, and provide us with new and easier ways to connect to each other and to many and different sources of knowledge and information. Many have argued that the new forms of media and technology have directly changed the ways that people relate to each other, individually and as members of groups, and to society (Turkle 2015, 2011; Meyrowitz 1985; McLuhan [1964] 1994), bringing us back to the central concerns of classic social theory.

On this I agree and will elaborate here: the rise of new forms of emotional display are, in fact, closely related to the age-old concern about the nature of modern social relationships described in the classic texts of social theory, a concern still addressed today but in new terms. Contained in these classic texts about changes in social relationships is the topic of the growth of "secondary groups" (Cooley [1909] 1962) or, more recently, the rise of "indirect," or mediated, relationships (Calhoun 1991a, 1992). From the classics to today, we find arguments about the loss of lasting face-to-face relationships and the social consequences of this loss. Put simply, "primary groups" (Cooley [1909] 1962, 25–31), the direct and interpersonal relations of "premier" forms of social organization and community, compete today with "secondary groups" as ways of associating with others; for modern individuals enter many and larger groups, organizations, and complex societies, where relationships are not face to face but indirect and deemed "impersonal." So described, these relations are not lasting but changing; they are typically based on practical or functional social roles of the workplace or society, in contrast to the personal and direct relations of social actors of "premodern" industrial societies. "Modern political and economic affairs are distinguished by the increasing frequency, scale, and importance of indirect social relationships" (Calhoun 1991a, 102).

Calhoun's extensive work on this topic of changing types of social relationships (1992, 1991a, 1988, 1980) uses "indirect" as a principal way of describing what Cooley and other early sociologists wrote about as "secondary relations," the changing human relations in modern industrial societies. Calhoun's indirect relations are "mediated" for they depend on some type of information-processing technology, technologies typically linked to modern and postmodern complex organizations.

This theme is found in another now-classic work on nineteenth-century nationalism (Anderson [1983] 1991), which argues that *the idea and experience of belonging to the (modern) nation* is one that is *mediated or communicated through media* that allow for the development of the nation as an "imagined community" (6). The nation is "imagined" not because it is false or unreal; rather it is constructed out of popular forms of communication that enable large numbers of people to experience nation-ness, to acquire a sense of identity with others, and to experience that they belong to a community with them. The modern nation is *imagined* because the members of even the smallest nation will never know most of their fellow members, meet them, or even hear of them, yet in the minds of each lives the image of their communion. [emphasis in original] (6)

The newly emerging nation-states of the late eighteenth and nineteenth centuries belong to the era of "print capitalism" (Anderson [1983] 1991, ch. 3): the printing of newspapers and pamphlets, for example, set down conditions for ideas and images to shape peoples across large geographical areas and to find common influence in these images and reports. Initially, the printing of the newspaper and the modern novel, for example, were cultural forms of and for a mass readership, providing conditions for peoples to "think" the nation, an entity imagined as a "deep, horizontal com- radeship," and to do so over vast spans of space and time. Modern printing, along with the impetus it received from capitalist forces, created new "mass monoglot reading publics" (Anderson [1983] 1991, 43).

This idea, at least in its broadest outlines, was acknowledged as early as the 1830s by Tocqueville in his chapter on newspapers ([1840] 1990, 111), who also saw newspapers as providing a new way for citizens to unite when they "are no longer united . . . by firm and lasting ties." A central concern of Tocqueville's work, one he shared with classical sociology, was the inevitable "disunity" of modern democracies. Newspapers made possible a new form of social unity in this era of democratic individualism: "This can be ... effected only by means of a newspaper; nothing but a newspaper can drop the same thought into a thousand minds at the same moment."

Anderson's argument is based on different historical presuppo- sitions than Tocqueville's about modern nations' relationships to capitalism and the nation's relation to printing. Anderson examines how the modern novel and the newspaper, for example, drew from new understandings of time and space, relative to those of antiquity and the aristocracies before the modern democratic era of industrial capitalism.

Anderson singles out as culturally significant the nation's capacity to provide a particular and new form or "*style* of continuity," one, he argues, made necessary by the waning notion of eternal salvation in the modern age, the end of the age of the religious community, and the dynastic realm ([1983] 1991, 11). Nations, these new "eternal" forms, "loom out of an immemorial past and, still more important, [nations] glide into a limitless future" (11–12). The idea of *the nation* serves to reposition the modern individual within a secular temporal order and to provide worldly categories, such as modern notions of evolutionary progress, national mission, or national destiny. Each of us is part of an imagined community that is experienced as eternal and our world is unimaginable without *the nation*, a construct of relatively recent heritage.

In the preface to *Imagined Communities* ([1983] 1991), Anderson asks, "Who would have thought that the storm blows harder the farther it leaves Paradise behind?" Described in the early 1990s, these ferocious "storms" refer to the most recent nationalist explosions that followed upon the end of the Soviet Union. Anderson's evocation of "paradise" refers to his claim concerning the roots of nationalism in secular cultures of today and the recent past: "The eighteenth century marks not only the dawn of the age of nationalism but the dusk of religious modes of thought ... the Enlightenment and rational secularism ... [the] disintegration of paradise" (11). The nation-as-community belongs with what we call "kinship" and "religion," not with "liberalism" or "fascism," or what we understand as "ideological forms" (5). Nationalism is to be understood against the vast cultural systems that preceded it historically (the religious community and the dynasty), which gave to their inhabitants a place, a destiny, a lineage, a cosmology. Nationness arouses "deep attachments" (4) and depths of feeling: national identities are fraught with emotions about belonging, about resistance, about brotherhood and sisterhood, about individual and collective identity.

As Calhoun has demonstrated, these ideas and sentiments about the nation were vital to modern political and cultural development, for they paralleled the idea of modern persons as individuals. The idea of the nation is temporally one and the same as the idea of the individual (see chapter 2 above, on modern identity); persons and nations are each unitary and integral ("indivisible") and, at the same time, self-sufficient, self-contained, and self-actualizing. Each (nation and individual) possesses a distinct character, a collective experience, and a destiny (Calhoun 1997, ch. 2; 1994, 1993a). The identification of these qualities, attributes, and capacities helps us to understand how the discourse of nations can evoke claims of loyalty and attachment, and in ways that override those of family, group, and region: the nation is me and I am the nation, of course, not always and for everyone, but effectively, it is so. *The nation is an attachment built on the identity of the modern individual; the nation is also the collectivity of individuals, united in sameness, in equality, in liberty.* Contained in Calhoun's discussion of the mirroring ideas of nation/individual is the remarkable claim (1993a, 396) that the modern notion of the individual is "the most decisive idea behind nationalism" or national identity. Put differently, modern individualism (see chapter 2 above) is what holds modern societies together, an irony not lost on Durkheim; individualism is "a solvent of community" today (Taylor 2004, 18).

A related topic, unexplored here, is the common practice of *personifying* the nation—representing, in image and song, icon and symbol, the nation as a person. I am thinking of Uncle Sam, an image (first used during the War of 1812) of patriotic emotion expressed and attached to a single individual. Another famous example is France's Marianne, a republican symbol and an icon of liberty and democracy. One sees Marianne in virtually every town hall and court of law in France. This practice—personification—may explain, in part, how nations can be thought of and portrayed for modern individuals and how these national representations can also serve us as we project onto them our national sentiments and emotions, especially at times of war and national crisis.

That the nation is an attachment built on the identity of the modern individual has far-reaching implications for understanding not only the centrality of nineteenth-century nationalism in the modern era and its likely persistence today as a prototype of identity in the face of globalization processes. In fact, because the idea of the nation is so fundamental to both modern and postmodern political consciousness and doctrine (Kedourie [1960] 1994), to people's identities, to ways of organizing our sociopolitical practices, and to our entire way of imagining our collective past, present, and future, because of the nation's preponderance in modern consciousness and its capacity to serve as a powerful collective representation of both "community" and of ourselves, because of all this, the nation has historically served as the prototype of all collective movements that have the capacity to stir emotions and loyalties and to garner "feelings of belonging," whether lasting and consequential or insubstantial and fleeting. This thesis rejects the view of nationalist sentiments and other emotions of masses and mass movements as expressions—regressive, primitive, natural—that are features of countermodern impulses as Foucault (1984, 39) has referred to the continuing struggle of the "attitudes" of modernity and countermodernity.

Accordingly, what I call "mass emotions" and mass movements are phenomena best understood in relation to the idea and the range of emotions and sentiments belonging to the era of the modern nation: not a mere collectivity, but the embodiment of a community for the modern individual, a way of belonging, what we call today an "identity." Writing about German nationalism at the time of the Great War, one contemporary historian (Eksteins 1989, 195–6) asserts:

> The individual was not just a particle within a utilitarian
> association called society; the ... individual *was* the nation ... And
> the nation was simply "a higher human being."

Those historians and social scientists whose arguments are compatible with Anderson's about the nation-states of the nineteenth century argue that these nationalisms and the related movements of fascism in Italy and Germany were *modern social movements* and belonged to the era of democratic (mass) politics[1] and its popular press, including its dissemination of photo and newsreel, as photography became part of the daily press and newsreels part of what publics viewed at the movies.

Eric Hobsbawm (1994, 117), for example, notes that fascism existed by "mobilizing masses from below" and "belonged to the era of democratic and popular politics, which traditional reactionaries deplored. Fascism gloried in the mobilization of masses and maintained it symbolically in the form of public theatre—the Nuremberg rallies, the masses on the Piazza Venezia looking up to Mussolini's gestures on his balcony ... as also did Communist movements." The element of public theater in the generation and display of emotions figures significantly in the study of these modern collective forms, as they do today in the new era of mass media.

There were other cases of mass movements and popular enthusiasms belonging to the age of modern nationalism. In fact, it was after the eighteenth century that social movements became vehicles of *popular politics* throughout the world (Tilly 2004). These mass or popular movements have also been interpreted as *mediated or communicated* by popular books and pamphlets and, later, by other media (Tilly 2004, 84–9). This suggests that both secular and religious movements of the modern era might draw from the same cultural dispositions in which they occur.

The case of Thérèse of Lisieux, who lived from 1873 to 1897, and the popular uprisings in France after her death have also been cited as modern mass enthusiasms. Uprisings on her behalf began with the publication of her autobiography in 1898, spreading to other nations where her book and story were distributed.[2] There are some parallels in this case to the apparitions that took place in the town of Lourdes, France, first witnessed by the peasant girl

Bernadette Soubirous in 1858, a half century before. But closer examination finds the case of Bernadette of Lourdes to be unlike that of Thérèse, who left a powerful and popular printed word after her death. By contrast, Bernadette left neither word nor text (R. Harris 1999, 161ff.). The social and spiritual impact of the child-saint Thérèse was personal and emotional and disseminated in print form; Bernadette's legacy was largely the shrine at Lourdes, the most famous in modern Christendom. A history of Lourdes by Ruth Harris (1999) examines its development within the context of French modern history and politics, modern medical practice, and popular pieties of the day.

Cases such as these popular religious movements raise questions about which classes, communities, and groups were moved to collective action—questions that require nothing short of a reconstruction of events in order to assess the motives, feelings, and structures of the groups involved; and, then, there is the comparison of these movements with other movements. Were they "social movements" at all (Small 1897; Tilly 2004, 1994)? In the United States and Europe, some popular pieties of intense religiosity were linked to the events of the world wars; I am thinking of Saints Jude and Thérèse as well as the popular and widespread pieties in the United States of immigrant Catholics who were devoted to these saints (e.g., see Orsi 1996). Another interesting case is that of Bernadette, whose nine-teenth-century story—when it was retold by Franz Werfel in the 1940s—evoked mass interest and enthusiasm in France and the United States.

Franz Werfel, the émigré author of both the novel and the film *The Song of Bernadette*, has been described as "a writer who registered every trend and tremor" of the extraordinary era from the turn of the century to the end of World War II. The English translation of Werfel's novel about this Catholic saint and her apparitions was published on May 11, 1942. Its US publisher and literary agent predicted a modest reception at best for this spiritual story of miracles; no one was prepared for its extraordinary popular success. In July 1942 it was selected by the Book of the Month Club as the "most important new book on the American market" (Jungk 1987, 201):

> The Song of Bernadette became one of the greatest hits in American
> publishing history . . . . Mass-media furor reached its peak
> in June 1942.

This remarkable coming together of the mass appeal of the story of religious apparitions in the time of war, when "American nationalism [was] in full flower" (Jungk 1987, 199), suggests a field of inquiry unexplored. Yet popular spiritual movements, in this case at least, seem to have emerged within the same social universe where the strong feelings associated with nationhood developed.

One study suggests that religious and spiritualist movements marked by intense emotionality belong to the history of *modern* religious (Protestant) evangelical movements. In his now-classic study of religious "enthusiasms," Ronald Knox (1950) suggests an affinity between these intensely emotional movements and other contemporary movements: "At what sources do they feed ... ?" he asks, "these torrents which threaten, once and again, to carry off our peaceful countryside in ruin?" (578). A more recent study (Washington 1993) views these matters with more humor and, surely, more objectivity than Knox, pointing out that the century of nationalisms was also the great age of independent spiritual teachers. Yet, in some cases, Washington points out, the American and British taste for spiritualism and spiritualist movements coincided with the rejection of nationalism and the embracing of pacifism and types of mysticism (Washington 1993, ch. 17).

The emotional intensity observed in a range of modern social movements, uprisings, and crowds draws upon this communal prototype of the nation: mass audiences, spectators, throngs gathered around modern-day heroes and stars, and popular enthusiasms surrounding saints, especially "saints of the people," as Thérèse of Lisieux was called. These movements shared an emotional intensity fostered by the consciousness of belonging to a large or vast communion of individuals, beings who share a faith or an identity as individuals with a common object, a shared destiny, a mass of individuals united in time and space whose individualities merge in a moment of belonging to and participating in an idea and ideal of themselves. In masses and crowds these intense emotional displays may be fleeting, but they are built upon and draw from the only vast community of individuals we know: *the nation, a unity that affirms the dynamic individual* of the modern era. Put differently, what are called "collective emotions" (von Scheve and Salmela 2014; von Scheve and Ismer 2013) of the modern era draw from the beliefs and images of the nation-as-community made up of individuals, sharing both a common object (the nation) and an identity of belonging.

When I read accounts (Berg 1998; Eksteins 1989) and see films of the crowds stirred by the solo flight of Charles Lindbergh, that solitary and heroic figure, and his landing in Paris in May 1927 (see "Lindbergh's Atlantic Flight ... " 2014), I am immediately struck by its mass features—crowds stirring similarly across nations and cities—and the "human tidal wave" that met him on the landing fields and the crowds dancing in the streets, not only of Paris but of Berlin, Amsterdam, Tokyo, London, New York. One is also struck by the man himself and the event as a national symbol, something Lindbergh himself understood. This modern-day boy-hero epitomized each of us and our nation.

His first stop after landing in Paris was at the Tomb of the Unknown Soldier at the base of the Arc de Triomphe; he himself became a symbol of the "high courage and dash of young America" (Berg 1998, 170). On the night after his landing in Paris, the "Star Spangled Banner" was played in all New York theaters before the overtures. The examples are legion. In his own words, "I was astonished at the effect my successful landing in France had on the nations of the world. To me, it was like a match lighting a bonfire" (Berg 1998, 135). This conflagration "transformed the 25-year-old 'boy' into the most famous man on earth," making him one of our first creations of mass media—simultaneously a figure of the democratic masses and a national hero.

An additional example from another social world entirely, Hollywood: Lindbergh had a kind of predecessor, surely not a hero, but a funny fellow of worldwide fame—Charlie Chaplin's Little Tramp—who, a little more than a decade before, in the first months of the Great War, became a masterful and unforgettable image. He was also called "the most famous man on earth," an appellation referring to his fame on the screen and his worldwide popularity. He was a figure who told the American working classes, in particular, a story of their own exploitation at the hands of the factory bosses and the ruling class. Charlie's tramp found his way into "the hearts of the great mass audience" (D. Robinson 1985, 145). Chaplin first discovered this in 1916 when crowds met him at every train stop from California to New York.

These two figures—Lindbergh and The Little Tramp—evoked both collective identification and individual feeling. It could also be claimed that the two became objects for "discovering" (or reinventing) national identities: Chaplin, as an actor, evoked a fascination with his "racial" origins, which, in a time when American anti-Semitism prevailed, aroused fears and suspicions about his being "Jewish." Reporters asked him repeatedly about this. He was also a target for Nazi anti-Semitism and his film "Gold Rush" was banned in the early years of the Third Reich (D. Robinson 1985). Chaplin disturbed the nationalist publics he attracted and whose racist fears he aroused. Were these fears appeased, in any way, by the sentiments and sentimental feelings fans gave him, offerings to Chaplin in the figure of The Little Tramp?

Even the accounts of Thérèse's followers and hagiographers were replete with "nationalist" discourse and imagery: Thérèse was said to have "a special attraction for valiant and virile hearts for warriors and soldiers, especially those in foreign places and in trenches ... [She] makes us dream of fatherland" (Society for the Propagation of the Faith 1924), and St. Thérèse was known to be popular among the French soldiers in the trenches (R. Harris 1999, 161).

At this point I should provide some disclaimers. My interest in religious and spiritualist movements is not in the least in pursuing some pseudo-religious basis to modern nationalisms. Nor am I trying to uncover some elemental psychological substrate to modern social movements. Rather I am asking: *what, if anything, might these two forms of collective phenomena (one spiritual and one political, both affiliative, both intensely believed and felt) reveal about distinctive modern predispositions, particularly feelings of belonging and identity?*

As a preliminary approach I am calling for a delineation of the social *behaviors, cultures* (common practices, values, norms, media), and *collective emotions* that stirred various types of crowds and masses within modern social settings (see these terms in von Scheve and Ismer 2013, 3). But I am also suggesting here that, in the transmission of knowledges and images of collective behaviors on screen through film, collective emotions can be further generated across space and time, as in the case of Lindbergh's landing in Paris.

Based on these modern-day examples, from the imagined communities of nation-states to popular uprisings coextensive with nationalism and other later mass enthusiasms (Lindbergh and The Little Tramp), my working proposition is that *mass emotions* and its twin concept *mass audiences* are only understandable if we study them as produced and communicated through media that allow for the development of these imagined communities and their shared emotional objects (whether nation, soldier, hero, saint) or the shared emotional symbols and iconography of these (flag, war monument, religious shrine, saint's or hero's photo, or moving image). These national objects and the cultural practices associated with them (monuments and veterans parades, the flag and the singing of the national anthem, the young hero Lindbergh and the films of him at the Tomb of the Unknown Soldier) are where emotions of patriotism and belonging emerge and are known for what they are. These objects and practices teach us how these emotions are collectively thought and known to be and how they are supposed to be felt and expressed. The cultural theory of emotions, identified in chapter 1 above, *conceives of emotion as inseparably part of a social object* (Parkinson and Manstead 2015; McCarthy 1989b); emotion includes the consciousness we have of what we feel, what we make of these feelings, and the values we attach to these feelings. The cultural landscape of modern nationalism, how people imagined themselves as part of an imagined community with others like them, their identities, and their feelings of pride and belonging, their willingness to die for the nation—all of these and more—are part of the emotions and feelings themselves. We observe them at work in many forms of collective cultural practices.

As Anderson ([1983] 1991, xiii–xiv) argued about the modern nation, communication media ("print capitalism") transformed the *spatial* and *temporal* organization of social life so that the idea and experience of nation-ness could develop, shaping peoples across vast territories. In the process, Cooley's "primary group relations," or face-to-face everyday life encounters, came to exist (they are never entirely replaced) alongside of new and emerging types of social relations, those with individuals and groups who are distant or absent and, in some cases, social relations with others known and felt as "close," but never known face-to-face.

This new type of social relationship—one "constructed" today by postmodern mass media—is described by many writing about the effects of mass media on social relation and on identities.[3] These studies include changes in people's experiences of space and time, their experiences of "simultaneity," and their experiences of these mediated human relations as "close" and "personal"—topics that have important implications for collective emotions. Each of these will be addressed in what follows.

John Thompson's (1995) well-known argument, in a work of social theory, is that several technical changes with printing and "electrical codification of information" brought about profound changes in the culture of modernity and postmodernity. Together, these changes, extending from the fifteenth to the twentieth century, constitute the "mediatization of culture" (46), which, in time, becomes "extended mediatization" (110) or media's increasing self-referentiality, an argument central to the thinking of another social theorist writing on mass media, Niklas Luhmann (2000).

Thompson explains the significance of "extended mediatization" this way (1995, 110): "Media messages commonly refer to other media messages or to ends reported therein," and these become part of the processes of communication and reception themselves. To understand media communication is to see the implications of the *self-referential nature of communication technologies*: we get news stories about stories; we get photo journalism accounts of persons involved in disasters; we get photos and films of a tornado weather forecast as we watch films of tornados tearing through Iowa ten years before; we get videos of baseball players from the past as we watch baseball players and fans now, playing in the same stadium. During the horrific 9/11 event, as it took place, we watched films of the planes going into the twin towers of the World Trade Center in New York City as we simultaneously watched the towers collapse in "real time."

But individuals also insert themselves into these processes and digital chains. They "appropriate" (Thompson 1995, 42–3) media information, reports, photos, films, and stories as they are viewed or heard; these, in turn, are transmitted to others near and close who, in turn, comment on the stories and photos, offering additional frames and contexts of meaning. Think of Facebook, Instagram, Twitter, and texting today. The process of people's appropriating media stories and events means that we make them our own and experience them as "mine" or "ours" by posting them on social network sites, texting them to others, offering a brief "Like" or "Reply," or making extended textual comments on blogs, posting comments about media events or posting others' "pics" (the current word for photos posted on Internet sites), which, in principle, are not our own but are experienced as mine or ours by our appropriation of them. All of this takes place without reference to the location of interlocutors. But the interlocutors typically experience these processes as "simultaneous" and the relationship of their interlocutors as close.[4] For these reasons and others, the mass media constitute a domain of interaction that fosters a sense of closeness versus distance, even a "perception of intimacy," as a new standard for media events, personal revelation becomes part of our "national appetite" (Meyrowitz 1985, 179; Meyrowitz 2002).

When people appropriate media messages, they are also engaged in a process of *self-understanding* and *self-formation* (Thompson 1995), so that people experience the process as "personal" and "subjective." "I know my cell and other stuff are not mine really, *but it's me that does what I want to with them*," a student recently told me. This new arena of self-fashioning is one that takes place "severed from the spatial and temporal constraints of fact-to-face interaction" (Thompson 1995, 43; McCarthy 1996, 81–4).

Altheide (2014, 3, 55) describes the "pervasive mediation of social interaction," meaning that today's media serve not principally as resources for action and interaction but as people's *environments* for their action and interaction. These relations and our daily routines are increasingly *mediated* as we use and draw from and exchange images and stories from TV, emails, texts, Instagram, Twitter, Facebook, and so forth. In fact, it's difficult to think of relations today that are untouched by "mediation." Actions like watching TV, using the Internet, or listening to the radio are mediated experiences, and they do not even require specific locations (like the living room or car) anymore; messages, shows, and images come to us via numerous digital technologies like smartphones, iPhones, and tablets.

This does not mean that people have removed themselves entirely from this face-to-face domain, but it points to something utterly new for many of us: we engage ourselves and others in these digital exchanges, and we also take up our lives in the domain of face-to-face roles and exchanges. We move between one domain and the other with relative ease, and yet these are different types of "realities."

One of them is a world of mediated objects, not directly known and sometimes rich with emotional imagery. The other reality is known in our everyday face-to-face exchanges with the other. The mediated self and its objects and friends have been pieced into the world of everyday life (Schutz and Luckmann 1973; Berger and Luckmann 1966). "Telefictive" experience (Wilson 2000, 80) stands alongside the "paramount" world of everyday life, not as a kind of fiction but as an integral part of my real experiences of self and others and world. The world online can also, we know, be experienced as "more real" than our "real lives" (Turkle 1995, 10). This raises more questions and reflections for emotion studies and contemporary studies of identity, like the following from an expert on media's effects (Turkle 1995, 26):

> It is computer screens where we project ourselves into our own dramas, dramas in which we are producer, director, and star … Increasingly we are able to draw in other people. Computer screens are the new location for our fantasies, both erotic and intellectual.

But these telefictive reels of messages and images running through me and my body are also emotional. This emotionality is a special feature of the mediatized world of images that are my constant companions in everyday life (Gitlin 2002). For one thing, watching TV and surfing the Internet are experiences that require neither special skills, as does reading, nor specific locations in which to do them. They are visual experiences. Meyrowitz (1985, 99) writes about the significant difference between the two modes of access of information and knowledge: electronic and visual versus print media. The former, on TV or Internet or cell phone, comes to us as personal and expressive, "more tied to the speaker," whereas print media are more readily communicated and received conceptually or as abstract issues, at a distance (see also K. Goldberg 2000). There is even some evidence that print versus visual signs evoke different parts of the human brain (the right hemisphere for linguistic, sequential data; the left for visual and spatial stimuli) (Meyrowitz 1985, 99n5, n6). Similarly, another media expert, Altheide (2014, 2), tells us that today media have become more "instantaneous, visual, and personal than in the past." Describing what he calls today's "media edge," Altheide states (2–3):

> Capturing images, being first with images; the focus on immediacy rather than meaning—and accuracy and context . . . . . It is the same logic of orchestrating the attention-grabbing visual of some action for the screen—the TV, the iPhone . . . that leads hundreds of local television news stations in the U.S. to "go live" with visuals of police chases in autos, often shot from hovering helicopters, before any meaningful information is obtained.

The visual world of media is intensely emotional and experiential, for it draws us closer in (or out, as the case may be) to itself through its sensational display of ordinary things and people and through its invention of extraordinary things, seen especially in the growth and appeal of "media spectacles" (Garber, Matlock, and Walkowitz 1993; Kellner 2003b). People in marketing, sales, design, and mass media already know this: how to make products and routines "delightful" (Altheide 2014, 5–6); how to create real "emotional connections" with our users; how to understand and appeal to our customers' and clients' "experiences" (*Revel Foundry* 2015).

Returning to the theme of "social relations" with which I opened these reflections, many refer to today's social relations as "indirect" (Calhoun 1991a, 1992) or "distant," in contrast to the older close relations that were more typically face-to-face (Cooley's "primary relations"). But these descriptions are inadequate to capture the social meanings today of "close" and "distant." Put differently, we no longer have cultural dispositions to render distance as a *social good*. I refer to social distances between individuals, between groups, between spectators and participants, between mourners and the mourned, between authorities and us. In its place there is an urge, indeed, a yearning, built into our mediated world and ourselves to get close to others and to things, to "eclipse" the distances of hierarchy and difference, to rid ourselves of formality.[5] This urge to get close to others and to things suggests a readiness, on our part, to seek out new ways of belonging and new ways of making and remaking "public life"—in politics, the arts, schooling and learning, parenting, friendship. Meyrowitz calls this newly emerging standard of relations "reciprocal informality" (1985, 32; see also Meyrowitz 2002; Wouters 1992; Boyd 2014, ch. 8) and refers to Richard Sennett's *The Fall of Public Man* (1977, 255), a work that describes today's "reigning belief" that "closeness between persons is a moral good."

My own reflections on "distance" and public life suggest a new and different experience of social order today, one described by the social philosopher Charles Taylor (2004) as a new "social imaginary" developing in our time (see chapter 3 above): new ways of people imagining themselves and their social lives with others. In fact, the very idea of this social imaginary is captured in the media phrase "direct access" and is derived in part from Benedict Anderson and others on the role of print capitalism. Today's social imaginary and ways of belonging take place at-the-same-time; they are marked by experiences of "simultaneity" (Anderson [1983] 1991; J. Thompson 1995, 32–3) in which people "interact" within mediated frameworks enabling instantaneous exchanges across vast geographical areas.

This entails a secular and modern understanding of time and space, one where we imagine "society" existing horizontally, an imagining without the mediations of hierarchies and distances. It is a secular imaginary where divine mediators (kings and priests) are missing and where "social action" takes place in the profane time of clocks and calendars. It is a "direct access" society where each of us is "immediate to the whole" (Taylor 2004, 157). In my thinking, not Taylor's, it is this social imaginary that today's mass media spectacles create, draw from, and reproduce, a human and global universe of simultaneous happenings that we, in principle, can access at any time. Think of the excitement of televised Olympic games and filmed New Year's Eve festivals hour by hour, world city by world city, or the collective sense of grief experienced when viewing the funeral of Princess Diana. "Anyone can access these events," a student told me. "There are no exclusions of literacy, race, or class." Even when my students watch new music-video releases, they see them *as everyone's without exclusion.*" Things are there—out there—for us all to access at any time. "Only connect."[6]

Today, the older social order of hierarchy and distance has been superseded by horizontal, direct-access societies (Taylor 2004, ch. 10). It is likely that if this idea has any merit at all, we might think of it as a process we are still witnessing, like the older idea of "modernities" (C. Geertz 1995, ch. 6). Integral to this imaginary are the effects of mass media and globalization on our experiences and imaginings of self and other, and of "society." Among these I can identify the new forms of modern "individualism" (chapter 2 above), the concept and experience of the person in the modern world (R. Williams [1976] 1985, 161–5; Calhoun 1994), a concept and experience changing throughout the modern and postmodern era (Elliot and Lemert 2006).

For from every standpoint today, modern "individuals" still seem to thrive and to assert their unique individuality, but as beings who imagine themselves as relational and "networked" rather than autonomous and separate from others and community: "Directness of access abolishes the heterogeneity of hierarchical belonging" (Taylor 2005, 160). Today we experience ourselves as free of mediations, whether those of the authorities of state, religion, or family. Because of this we imagine and experience ourselves as belonging to wider and wider communities. For some of us, identities of race and faith, gender and sexuality have superseded our identity as citizens. For others, *the nation* still reverberates in us as the first identity, while for others no single identity (not even nationhood) stands paramount or alone.[7]

The emotional intensity of the public and collective social performances that drew me to this study (chapter 1 above) now makes a kind of sense, and the role of mass media in these events is even greater than I suspected. I remain convinced that something "cultural" has been happening to change today's social relations and the particular "emotional cultures" (P. Stearns 1994) they draw from.

The sites where we witness the changing emotional cultures are in places to which we have to travel. It's a wider world that should deserve our careful attention, an argument made by some emotion researchers (Parkinson and Manstead 2015, 377; Parkinson, Fischer, and Manstead 2005). For the principal sites where we can observe the many collective events and stages that hold out to us the promise of excitement and "real emotion" are in public sites and public events.[8]

It is *out there* with others that we witness today a kind of emotional intensity, one where people imagine themselves in new types of communities-of-belonging: at sports arenas and music concerts, in city parks and streets, at the National September 11 Memorial and Museum in New York—places where people assemble to experience and to engage themselves and others in all kinds of happenings and events, where, like actors together on a stage, they know how to play the part. They know too that they are participants in events transmitted to them simultaneously on film and video. They also watch themselves as spectators and transmit messages and post photos and videos about what they are doing and feeling.

These are not the "crowds" of an earlier modernity, if they ever existed at all (McPhail 1991). For one thing, these new performances we engage in with others and the portable media technologies we carry with us "create private spaces in the midst of crowded" sites (Meyrowitz 1985, 324). There is no doubt that the emotions of these moments take on a larger life when these social actors attend these events while "at play" with their cell phones and video cameras. Even if we do not record these events on cell phone or video, our participation carries with it a consciousness that this is a *media event* and that we are participants in a vast social imaginary, a crowd where intense happenings are taking place.

Thus, as I attend a fireman's funeral in Cleveland, Ohio (Associated Press 2015), I am caught up in the intense emotions of the event, swept up into a mediatized image of the thousands of firefighters marching in this sad parade. I'm thinking now that what I'm watching might appear on YouTube and the nightly news. My intense emotions—sadness and excitement—as a spectator-participant do not reside in me or in those around me today as much as in the *social imaginary* that is playing in my head: the vast crowd of participants and onlookers that I feel part of, the sight of the flag-covered casket of the fallen fireman, the slow and uniform procession of firefighters and flags, and the piper's mournful tune "Going Home."

Afterword

Writing and Thinking about Emotions Today

As a sociologist, I have been trying to write about emotions for a very long time, trying again and again to state my argument as directly and as clearly as I can. This search for clarity and transparency in thought and expression, I now think, is a misplaced, even a mad sort of project because of the endless difficulties of nailing down anything about human emotions. In fact, I have come to see that my life's project of writing about emotions and the self, using the rational discourse of sociology, is one that exists in tension with human emotions themselves, which are decidedly opaque and elusive, not only to ourselves as human subjects but also to scientists and those in the humanities studying the emotions. Over these years of writing, I have also come to see much more clearly—as I set out to do—how our feelings and emotions are shaped by culture in all its complex aspects; but I have also come to see how emotions also act as forces in shaping what people think and believe about themselves and reality, an argument made by the late great emotions scholar, Nico Frijda and his colleagues (Frijda 2000; Frijda, Manstead, and Bem 1986).

In this book—my most recent attempt—I try again to make the case that the emotions, despite what we have been told by both marketeers and therapists, are most truly *social things*. I do not mean by this that the families and groups we belong to shape them or tell us how to feel and what feelings mean or how we are to manage them. Of course, I mean all of that. But I also mean more than that.

I mean that these precious elements of ourselves and our identities are one of the most vital ways that we can know ourselves, but that in doing this—knowing ourselves as feeling beings and as beings with feelings—we are always in continual contact with society: with languages of the self that we inherit from our social worlds; with collective ideas and images of what emotions are and how we are supposed to manage them and control them and express them. I also mean by this statement—emotions are social things—that society prompts us and rehearses us about how we are to think and to speak of emotions: *how much* we should or should not feel, *what* we should or should not feel; which feelings and emotions we should cultivate or control or repress; which emotions we are to keep secret from others and secret also from ourselves and which ones we are to admit to openly. Emotions are also social because they are closely linked to the many forms of personal and institutional secrecy. Emotions may be sources of authentic selfhood, as many of us believe today, but not all kinds of selfhood are welcomed and embraced by society. Put differently, we are a people, as Irving Howe (1967, 31) once wrote, "entranced with depths," especially our own. But we are not all entranced with the same human depths and emotional complexities. Some of our emotional depths get us into trouble and are the sources of ostracism, prejudice, and even violence.

In recent years my students tell me—with remarkable consistency—that emotions are the most real thing about us. They tell me this in courses that have almost nothing to do with emotions and identity. To put this conviction of theirs into academic terms, terms most familiar to me: *many young people I know and read and listen to believe that emotions are the closest thing we have to "nature" and to what is ours without social influence.* They think, too, that emotions are the "real-est" thing we can know about ourselves; they also say that they are fully aware of how much society influences each of us. But, despite social influence, these young people believe that their feelings and emotions remain relatively untouched by social influences. For these reasons, they tell me that emotions are the closest parts of them that are real and natural. Of course, I tell them that these ideas they have about emotions are beliefs, part of culture, their culture. We talk and argue a lot about this. I tell them that they are "essentializing" or "absolutizing" emotions. They tell me I think that everything is social. And they are right in saying so. From our talking and arguing I can report that both participants—me and them—thoroughly enjoy these discussions, because, after all, we agree that emotions are important and that emotions are, in important ways, our very own, an idea of not so long vintage in the modern West (Taylor 1989, 2004). And so we can get excited and emotional in these intensely felt conversations among relative strangers in a public classroom. This excitement is not part of our other discussions about other topics, only the emotions.

Of course, when my students speak of the reality of their emotional selves, they are also telling me about their beliefs about the importance of emotions, of being "real" and "authentic," a theme I have written about throughout these pages. I have tried here and in other writings (McCarthy 2009, 2002) to argue that today's self or identity is closely aligned with "authenticity": indeed, emotions today have become central to our quest for what we call authenticity. It is a culture whose origins have been traced to our Romantic past, where feelings and emotions speak to us about who we are, telling us the most vital things about ourselves. Authenticity, in this sense, is a particular language of the self, an intensely sentimental (suffused with emotion) type of discourse; it is a way of speaking about who I am, my identity, which in its postmodern manifestation is an intense experience (and pursuit) of myself as I truly am.

As I have developed these ideas about authenticity today and its continuity with its emotional and sentimental past, I also argue that authenticity has been changed and intensified by contemporary media culture. In a thoroughly media-saturated world the pursuit of authenticity—and the dramatization of the real versus the fake, the natural versus fabricated, the "real article" versus the phony—has become a cultural preoccupation. Indeed, "popular culture is obsessed with authenticity and awash with artificiality," as Mukerji (2007, 1) has convincingly argued, and this "obsession" is played out in a number of highly visible and intensely emotional cultural practices, from the worlds of sports, leisure, and entertainment to those of religion and politics.

So the central argument I have been making here concerns the special place of emotions in our contemporary culture. More than that, I've been saying that today we pursue an emotional life with a kind of intensity. This is because emotions are, *inter alia*, integral to who and what the postmodern self is. Feelings and emotions are keys for unlocking who I am, my authenticity, how I perceive and how I discover my "real self." As others have shown us, this was not always the case (Taylor 1989; Bell 1996; Illouz 2007; Reddy 2001; Trilling 1971). Rather, the conjunction of emotion and identity is a feature of a distinct postmodern culture of emotion, an everyday understanding, a vernacular speech-form. What is new, I think, is precisely this conception of emotion as something the self *has* that is peculiar to postmodern identity and its emotional culture, a dominant view of thought and feeling as "possessions of the individual" (Taylor 1989, Part II); thinking and feeling are "interiorized"; they are mine, as is personhood itself. But by having emotions (and "being emotional") I also mean that emotions are some of the most important ways that postmodern persons search for and discover their authenticity: their sense of who they really are. Feeling deeply and intensely alive—these are moments and experiences that say to us, "This is *me*! This is who I *really* am!" (Erikson 1968, 19, emphasis in original).

Emotions are social things: I also have tried to point out that despite what many others have said about modern societies being rational and instrumental, these societies also, and in distinct ways, provoke in us certain types of feelings. And by "emotion discourse" I mean the words for and descriptions of emotions, like guilt and anxiety, for example, that we moderns seem to excel at using. In fact, as I have also argued on these pages, we seem to be witnessing today an intensification of emotion discourse, of being emotional, and of telling others and ourselves that we are emotional and what that means. Often "being emotional" is not a good thing, like those family members and friends we call "drama queens," whom we judge as too dramatic (certainly "overacting") and too emotional and, maybe, too self-absorbed. Then again, we judge others as being "uptight" or reserved or inexpressive, because they lack that socially desirable trait of being open about how we feel and what we feel. Others we judge as "tight-assed" or inhibited or ungenerous in terms of sex or other favors. As these expressions from our everyday lives tell us, we are often making judgments about what emotional behaviors and expressions mean. And these judgments are part of our emotion discourse: a vocabulary of a sort, a vocabulary of words and meanings about emotions, whether anger or laughter or meanness or generosity—signs of emotions and the self. A case in point: we seem to have arrived at a point where being real and being authentic trumps other emotional behaviors; for example, in today's political discourse, the perception and meaning of authenticity may be out-distancing other desirable traits of our political leaders, like experience, decorum, honesty, and fairness.

My own idea about emotions—clearly one that is both personal (central to my life in the world for some time now) and professional (the academic topic that I have pursued for many years)—is that emotions are not so much my own as they are given to me from the various life-worlds in which I have traveled. Emotions are also vitally important as I cultivate an identity, that is, how I experience and articulate who I am. But I principally mean to say that emotions are part of the language I have inherited from my family, my social class, and the world of the United States in the second half of the twentieth century and into the twenty-first, where I have lived and belonged—a place with all its emphasis on psychiatry and its tales and lessons of "making it," a place where emotions have also been some of the main characters in my own pursuits of having and getting things, of being and becoming someone. In other words, wanting to be someone and becoming someone on the many terrains of life (intimacy, friendship, family, work, community, and so forth) takes feeling things, wanting things, fighting for things, and believing in things—and all of these are helped by owning up to the emotions we feel, that is, by being honest with ourselves and others about what we feel.

I have come to think that these ideas and standards about knowing and expressing emotions are part of today's emotional culture, but that may not be the case at all. It may be what some of us have come upon as a way to navigate the difficult terrain of our alienating and artificial culture and our fears about emotional emptiness.

By "emotional emptiness" I refer to the modern and postmodern theme (found in works of fiction and nonfiction alike, especially of social science) that emotions elude us, even as we know more about them, study them, talk about them as much as we do. This was another idea that drove me to study emotions, the notion that the emotions I felt were not my own, or despite my emotional pursuits and ideals that I never truly felt deeply at all, or that my life belied an emotional emptiness. I have come to accept these thoughts and experiences, and I have been enriched by the classical social thinkers who first wrote about this emptiness, especially Georg Simmel, who described the experience of loneliness in crowds and of the restlessness that comes to us from the overstimulation of daily life in modern cities. As I have said, my own pursuits of an emotional life and a life of emotions have come, in part, from this fear I had about my own emotional emptiness: that is to say, as many moderns have before me, that we fear that we have never lived at all, meaning that we have never felt anything deeply. This might mean that today's emotional pursuits draw from our (collective) experiences of emotional emptiness. In other words, we have so many emotional pursuits because we want to feel and to feel more.

Related to this idea of a collective emotional emptiness is an idea captured in an upbeat and happy song, "It's Only a Paper Moon," of 1933 and popular through the 1950s: a romantic song about the emotion of love as transformative of everything in our empty, artificial world. The song is about how love can change the trappings and stagecraft of paper and muslin into something significant, something real. "Paper Moon" speaks of loving and needing someone so much that the phoniness of our world no longer matters. The reality and the emotion of love make all inauthenticity disappear so that lies and staging matter no more. The lyrics also tell a story of how love changes everything into something else, a crazy and romantic idea that I have always thought was true. Based on the popularity of this theme—love's transforming quality—in this and other popular songs (Scheff 2011), I think that I am not alone in holding this belief. When I sing the song, I always hear the voice of Ella Fitzgerald in her great 1945 recording ("It's Only a Paper Moon" 2016); here's the first two sets of lyrics by E. Y. Harburg and Billy Rose (music by Harold Arlen):

> You say it's only a paper moon
> Sailing over a cardboard sea
> But it wouldn't be make-believe if you believed in me
> Yes, it's only a canvas sky
> Hanging over a muslin tree
> But it wouldn't be make-believe if you believed in me
> Without your love it's a honky-tonk parade
> Without your love it's a melody played in a penny arcade
> It's a Barnum and Bailey world
> Just as phony as it can be
> But it wouldn't be make-believe if you believed in me.

As I sing this song or when I sing it along with Ella, I know that some of the pleasure it gives me is from my playful acting and singing as if I were on a stage in front of an audience. And while I am not a very good actor or singer, the self-conscious happiness I feel when singing comes from this act of pretending to be like Ella—cool and seductive and happy in her talk of love. Also, as I sing, I become like Ella and I begin to believe even more what she is singing about: Ella is not just telling us a story, although she is doing that too. Ella has become—in the act of singing—someone in love whose world has become as real and as happy as she sounds. And I want to be like that and feel that too. Of course when Blanche Dubois in Tennessee Williams's *A Streetcar Named Desire* sings "Paper Moon," the song becomes a pathetic denial of the reality about to finally swallow up Blanche.

So there are songs and there are songs, as well as singers. Songs of light and darkness—and somewhere in between: my "Paper Moon"; the raw energy of the Stones proclaiming what a "gas" is "Jumpin' Jack Flash" with that spike in his head; or the madness of a nation singing the "Horst Wessel," the Nazi anthem to death and destruction, and marching to annihilation. To mention but a few . . .

And so I have come to the end of this latest venture. I leave you with this image of me or of any one of us singing and dancing along to the songs that surround us or the music we're plugged into that we carry around with us. Our everyday lives draw us inside ourselves, as the many critics of mass media argue. But, as I see it, much more important in this media revolution is that our mediatized world of images and sounds draws us outward to places and to people previously unimagined, to new communities, and to new worlds where both actors and "real people" beckon us to join them: on the sets of reality TV shows; on the sets of TV drug commercials, where old and young athletes tell us about the benefits of taking blood thinners, as they play a round of golf; on the living room sets of the soap operas we watch daily, where we meet people more real to us than our own relatives. These people and places beckon us and hold out to us fun and excitement and, sometimes, something more than that. They also hold out to us a sense that in being part of the reality of these public mediatized settings—memorial sites set up after a deadly house fire, a city street where someone risked her life to save a homeless man, the runway where a sports team arrives for a final world competition—we can catch hold of the *real feelings and emotions* that we have come to attach to these public stages and events. But there is surely more to all this excitement and emotion in public places.

But whatever makes these performances and spectacles more understandable, it is surely the fact that many of us live our everyday lives immersed in the information and imagery that beckon us to come along for the ride. Today's Wonderland is not discovered by tumbling down a rabbit hole. It's a stage or a movie screen that I can step up to or in to. These are the places—especially the spectacles of

entertainment, politics, sports, death and its memorials—that he
out to us the promise of real emotion.

A final note on method and theory. This is a work of interpretation not explanation, an exercise in what Clifford Geertz (2008, 17–20)
called the perspective of "interpretive anthropology." It is up to the
readers and my colleagues in emotions studies to decide if the
interpretation I have offered here is adequate to the subject matter.

In this book, I have offered several interpretations of some of
today's *emotional performances.* I have used various texts to assist me
in this task: among them, works of social theory on modern and
postmodern societies and identities; treatises and narratives about
modern individualism (an important piece of our inherited language
of the self); works by emotion scholars on today's emotional cultures;
studies of mass media. I have tried to paint a picture of what a cultural
sociology of emotions might look like, arguing for current changes in
both the prevailing emotional cultures and identities in our social
worlds today. The presupposition of this approach is that emotions
are inescapably part of "culture" (the word implies something unified
and whole that is actually disparate and multifarious). Emotions are
many things. Since they are "embodied," they are scrutinized by fields
of study like psychology, neurology, and physiology. My own
approach to this "embodiment" does not deny the importance of
these and other fields of study but argues that, whatever else emotions
are, they are part of history and culture. Since they do not exist and are
not felt apart from culture, it is a worthwhile venture to try to study
them this way. The truths about emotions are, then, contained in
these exercises of cultural interpretation.

Appendix A
Emotions, Psychology, and the Sociology of Knowledge

A few words on my own particular approach to emotion studies. While this is a work that can be located within "constructionist" approaches and cultural studies more generally, my own approach is indebted to contemporary studies in the sociology of knowledge, to interactionist social psychology (the tradition of G. H. Mead and the American pragmatists), and to studies of social identity inside and outside of sociology proper.

The sociology of knowledge traditionally examined the social and group origins of ideas, arguing that the entire ideational realm (knowledges, ideas, ideologies, mentalities) develops within the context of a society's groups and institutions. The sociology of knowledge has also been applied to the study of human psychology and to such topics as the social self and identity (Berger 1970, 1977; Farberman 1970). Peter Berger's theoretical model for applying the framework of the sociology of knowledge to the study of the psychological domain has influenced my early work in social psychology and emotions studies, particularly the project of linking various structural and cultural features of *modern* and *postmodern societies* to distinct emotional cultures: how modern notions of personhood—standards of human feeling and being, as well as the ideas and social categories that modern persons use to define and to interpret their experiences—can be understood as particular constructs or features of a *culture of modernity*.

As I argue in this book, we can extend this argument into the domain of the emotions, for example, arguing that certain features of postmodern selfhood can account for changes in the social meanings of emotions and emotional display (expression) in postmodern societies. Without question and as I argue here, the relatively new and growing digital environment is also an important new feature of today's collective psychology and its emotional cultures.

Emotional Lives can also be described as an argument for emotion studies that is both *cultural*—focused on cultural systems of meaning as the locus of human emotionality—and *historical*—arguing that sociocultural changes across time will, in turn, be registered in the domain of human sentiments and emotional experiences, although how precisely culture and experience change relative to each other is a matter to be investigated. The focus in each of the sections of this monograph is on the *experiences* that underlie a number of very public and social activities in today's world, in consumerism, mass media, the entertainment industries, leisure, and contemporary forms of memorializing events of death and devastation. It is my contention that a number of social arenas, such as the ones I describe here, draw from and presuppose (as well as reproduce) a distinct culture of selfhood and a distinct (modern and postmodern) form of emotionality that includes a distinct relationship to the body and its functions, an identifiable set of standards of emotional control and expression. In fact, many of these topics have already been identified by scholars with a history of modernity in its different phases. Sketched out briefly here, the topics examined have included the early modern period with its rules and new standards of "civility" and etiquette and an accompanying rise in self-consciousness about the artful process of self-presentation (Elias [1939] 2000; Greenblatt 1980); the eighteenth century rise of "sentimentalism" (Reddy 2001; Taylor 1989), an emotional regime that, in its full flowering, extolled emotions as both natural and morally good; and the development of nineteenth century "sentimentality," expressed in a Victorian reserve in matters of feelings—a reserve that struggled with the widely accepted view of the "vitality of feelings" (Gay 1984, 455).

In the years of writing this book—a writing that itself reflects the enormous academic and popular concern given to the emotions—its focus and method became clearer: *to identify various cases and sites where emotional display and cultural practice come together.* Part of my claim is that public manifestations of feeling and emotion, operating in different domains of public life, seem to have replaced earlier public behaviors marked by form, restraint, and decorum. Similarly, highly ritualized expressions of emotion and sentiment, such as those found in social courtesies and religious rituals, for example, have become more explicitly emotional and personal.

The perspective I am using examines the cultural systems (discourses as well as popular cultural forms like the mass media and all the digitized electronics we use daily) in which the emotions have—most recently—come into being *as something*, that is, as objects of experiences that *mean* something, and as a differentiated system of signs with which the self engages. I am asking, "What are the emotions today? What are today's standards, ideas, and precepts concerning how to feel and what to feel and what feelings mean?" And I am proposing here to answer these questions through an examination of certain cultural practices—a kind of method that looks on the outside for answers to what the emotions (inside) are and what they mean. Of course, I do not mean this literally (that emotions are inside us); I mean this figuratively, as I try to capture what emotions are in the everyday sense of things—*there*, in that domain, emotions are vital goods, interior possessions, housed inside us. I am asking, "How do today's very public emotional pursuits show us something about ourselves today and our emotions and what they mean?" This could be called a "hermeneutics of emotions": an interpretive reading of emotions as *cultural objects*, as signifiers of selves and selfhood today as they are played out in the very public domains of social life.

This is, of course, a very different kind of interpretation than the therapeutic one that dominates our culture today. In fact, a cultural model used to interpret emotions understands psychology itself and its therapeutic ethos as dominant components of modern culture (Illouz 2007). As my work progressed, it was to the work of Raymond Williams (1961, 48) that I turned again and again. As Williams has described a "structure of feeling" (see the opening here of chapter 1), I have tried to describe "emotions" today: what we think of them and how we respond to and interpret emotions—our own and others—is indeed a "very deep and very wide" matter, something vital to who we are collectively and what we know emotions to be and to mean.

APPENDIX B
Norbert Elias and the Making of Modern Inwardness

Despite the important differences in the methods of Norbert Elias and Charles Taylor—historical sociology and intellectual history, respectively—we are provided with historical descriptions on the making of modern "inwardness" and identity that are remarkably compatible. Furthermore, both authors argue that modern identity—in contrast to earlier historical forms of identity—is characterized by a distinct type of reflexive stance, a turning inward, a self-awareness or taking charge of ourselves; autonomous selfhood, a modern formation, requires a process of inwardness, becoming aware of ourselves so that we can objectify ourselves and take control of our thoughts, actions, and emotions (Taylor 1989, 174–6). Elias's [1939] 2000) *The Civilizing Process* is an account of the historical development of the "civilized" person in modern European societies, particularly the self-controlled, privatized, autonomous, and self-conscious individual—arguments, as we shall see, that are clearly related to an emotional portrait of modern selfhood or identity and its distinct culture of emotions.

Elias's thesis is that the history of Western society from the late Middle Ages to the nineteenth century represents a gradual transformation in people's ideas (and later, their feelings and behaviors) concerning manners and bodily propriety, changes associated with a number of factors, particularly (in its early phases), the importance of court societies with their codes of behavioral and emotional deportment. Central to this transformation were decisive changes in the feelings of shame, repugnance, and embarrassment that attended a wide range of bodily functions, such as eating, spitting, nose-blowing, urinating, and defecating.

This history of manners can be read as a history of a word and a concept, "civilization": first, the *courtoisie* or courtliness of the Middle Ages; next, the *civilité* of the Renaissance through the early sixteenth century; and, finally, *civilisation* of the late eighteenth and nineteenth centuries. The words signify moments in the long-term process of social and psychological development. Each indicates different standards of conduct within a sequence of change. In its fullest development *civilization* refers to Western nations' consciousness of themselves as bearers of a stage of human and social development, a consciousness of their own superiority in their morality, law, and scientific and artistic achievements. The development of this idea (one today that has undergone extensive critical social and political commentary as both "local" and ideological) coincided with a long-term trend: *affect and impulse came under increasingly tighter social and personal controls, and shame thresholds advanced accordingly.*

Elias sees a transition to a new and different standard of behavior introduced in *De civilitate morum puerilium* (On civility in children) by Erasmus of Rotterdam, published in 1530—a standard represented by *civilité*, which acquired its meaning during the second quarter of the sixteenth century when chivalry and the unity of the Catholic church were disintegrating. This highly influential treatise (it had over one hundred and thirty editions and appeared in many translations) reveals a new sensitivity about how people should conduct themselves in society, extending beyond table manners to bodily propriety—carriage, dress, and facial appearance and gestures. While many of the earlier directives from courtesy books are repeated by Erasmus, one detects a new way of seeing, of distancing oneself from what one sees. There is a greater sensitivity to how one appears to others. Erasmus's own precepts reveal a careful eye, and he exhorts his readers to be observant. Civility, as Elias notes, is removed from mere courtesy and closely bound up with a manner of seeing. "Look about you," Erasmus urges, "and pay attention to people, their feelings, and their motives." For Elias, this signifies a critical moment in the history of the civilizing process: human behavior takes on a different character seen in the increased tendency to observe oneself and others. According to this standard, "people moulded themselves and others more deliberately than in the Middle Ages" (68). As the demand for self-control was raised, controls became more internal and unconscious. In this way, Elias speaks of certain affect-expressions becoming, in time, "privatized" or "forced into the 'inside' of individuals, into 'secrecy'" (121).

→ the "unconscious"

Rebellion against civilisation therefore involves deprivatisation. :)

Notes

CHAPTER I

1. For a seminal essay on the repositioning of the academic disciplines, see Clifford Geertz's "Blurred Genres: The Refiguration of Social Thought," in *Local Knowledge* (New York: Basic Books, [1983] 2000b), 19–35. For another interpretation of the changes in the disciplines, see V. Y. Mudimbe, ed., *Open the Social Sciences: Report of the Gulbenkian Commission on the Restructuring of the Social Sciences* (Stanford, CA: Stanford University Press, 1996).

2. The diverse and sometimes conflicting approaches to the study of emotions in social science has included those of the positivists (Kemper 1978, 1987, 1990, 2011), interpretive sociologists (Denzin 1984), and interactionists (Franks and McCarthy 1989). Sociology's theories of emotion, largely borrowed from psychology, have also drawn from a diversity of psychological models, including social constructionism (Averill 1980; Gergen 1985; Harré 1986), psychoanalytic and psychodynamic psychology (Scheff 1979), and behaviorism (Brady 1975; Ekman 1982; John D. Baldwin 1985).

3. Not to overstate, there are studies where the emotions are not considered as "constructs" but viewed analytically as part of cognitive social psychology (e.g., Reddy 2001) or examined within a structural or organizational lens, such as in Eva Illouz's early work.

4. Thomas Kuhn's *The Structure of Scientific Revolutions* (Chicago: University of Chicago Press, [1962] 1970) laid down the principle that the natural sciences are "paradigm determined"; Robert Friedrichs (1970) argued the same for sociology. Roland Robertson (1992), Margaret Archer (1988), and Diana Crane (1994) have argued that the concept of culture has only recently become central to sociology's reasoning.

5. In McCarthy (1996, ch. 1), I offer some historical and cultural arguments for this "cultural turn." For commentaries on this turn to culture in sociology, see Wuthnow (1987), Robertson (1992), Crane (1994), Mukerji

and Schudson (1991, ch. 1), and Swidler and Arditi (1994). For a now-classic formulation on the concept(s) of culture in social science, history, and anthropology today, see Sewell's (1999) review and critique.

6. See, for example, R. S. Perinbanayagam's linguistically based writings on the social self (1982, 1991, 2000, 2011), Kenneth J. Gergen's *The Saturated Self* (1991), and John Shotter and Kenneth Gergen's *Texts of Identity* (1989). For an important *theoretical* contribution on the social self, see Norbert Wiley's (1994) synthesis of Peirce's and Mead's semiotic theories of the self.

7. The phrase "attitude of analysis" is Paul Ricoeur's (1986, 255–6). An early and leading proponent of social science's semiotic concept of culture is Clifford Geertz, particularly his book *The Interpretation of Culture* ([1973] 2000a, 14; cf. ([1983] 2000b). Cultural studies was originally given shape through the works of Raymond Williams, whose idea of "culture" is described here (1981, 12–13).

8. Since the period when emotion studies developed in these disciplines, the study of emotions has continued to flourish in the social and psychological sciences. See, for example, sociologist Jack Katz's *How Emotions Work* (Chicago: University of Chicago Press, 1999), sociologists Jonathan Turner and Jan Stets's *The Sociology of Emotions* (New York: Cambridge University Press, 2005), and the cognitive psychologist Keith Oatley's *Emotions: A Brief History* (Oxford, UK: Blackwell, 2004), as well as the large body of works in the field of psychology called "affective science."

9. Among them I include Rom Harré (1986, 1991), Deborah Lupton (1988), and Simon Williams (2001, see especially, 45–50).

10. I am borrowing Marshall Sahlins's terms from his influential *Culture and Practical Reason* (Chicago: University of Chicago Press, 1976), 123.

CHAPTER 2

1. Others who have made similar observations include: Lupton, Barbalet, and Williams; cf. Kemper 1990, 3–4.

2. In the United States and English-speaking North America and Europe's middle classes.

3. Heller, Sosna, and Wellbery 1986; Calhoun 1994, 9–36; *The Hedgehog Review* 1999.

4. See C. Stearns and P. Stearns 1986, 15n33 on S. Tomkins.

5. Daniel Bell 1996, 48; see also 46n10.

6. This is the opening line of Giddens's *Runaway World* (2000, 19). But there are any number of other similar pronouncements on modernity across the disciplines with which I identify here, such as Irving Howe's (1967) essay, "The Idea of the Modern" and Marshall Berman's *All That is Solid Melts into Air* (1982). For the contributors to the collection *Modernity and Identity* (1992) modernity "is a matter of *movement*, of flux, of *unpredictability*." (See the editors' "Introduction: Subjectivity and Modernity's Other.")

7. Theories of identity in the social and psychological sciences came into use in the United States in the 1950s in an age when discussions about the relationship of "individual" and "society" became prominent in academic as well as popular discourse; "identity" was part of an idiom that sought to explain something about the differences of "Americans" relative to their immigrants, Negroes, and Jews in the postwar era and its critics of "mass society" (Gleason 1983). For a history of the use of "race" and "national character" in American social science, see Daniel Bell's ([1980] 1991, ch. 9) "National Character Revisited." Craig Calhoun makes the point that modern social theory effectively suppressed "difference" through its emphasis on "individualism" (1994, preface). Modern identity (e.g., "individualism") operated both to articulate and to suppress political struggles for recognition and for "difference" in America. For a related discussion on the rise of the modern vocabulary of "individual" and "society," see Raymond Williams's *Culture and Society* ([1958] 1983) and *The Long Revolution* (1961).]

8. I am referring to the arguments of Raymond Williams in *Culture and Society, The Long Revolution*, and *Keywords*; refer as well to Swart (1962), Lukes (1973), and Heller, Sosna, and Wellbery (1986).

9. This is the well-known argument of Peter Berger on "identity" found in a number of works including, *The Social Construction of Reality, Facing Up to Modernity*, and his 1965 essay on psychoanalysis and the essay (1970) on identity as a problem in the sociology of knowledge.

10. The concept of "life-world" comes from Alfred Schutz (e.g., see Schutz and Luckmann 1973). In the works of Peter Berger this concept is applied to problems of identity and modernization (1967); see, in particular chapter 3 in *The Homeless Mind* (P. Berger, B. Berger, and Kellner, 1973).

11. In this regard see also Niklas Luhmann (1998, 2): "The modernity of society is determined by the meaning it assigns to the self-determining individual."

12. In political treatises from Marx's *Grundrisse* to Karl Polanyi's *The Great Transformation* ([1944] 2001) these themes of "autonomy" are, however differently, examined.

13. Modern sociology has consistently offered in its own narratives of "society and the individual" an ambivalent (sometimes, contradictory) account of *social action* and *human agency*, one where its own "naturalistic logic" operates in conflict with its narrative of "human agency," a sociological category that points to individual freedom, autonomy, and voluntarism. Sociology remains "divided over the relative import of action and structure" (Somers and Gibson 1994, 43; cf. Alexander 1982, 98).

14. Trilling (1971, 19–20) concurs, late sixteenth and early seventeenth century, referring to Frances Yates and Zeveder Barbu. See note on p. 174.

15. On inwardness, see also Lionel Trilling's (1971) reference to the interior self; DeJean (1997, ch. 3); Gay (1995); and Brennan (2000, ch. 3).

16. Taylor uses "subjectivism" (1989, 188) as others have also used it, to describe a distinctive feature of the modern identity. For example, Peter Berger has used it, inter alia, in his discussion of the "pluralization of life-worlds" (1963; cf. P. Berger, B. Berger, and Kellner 1973). Arnold Gehlen's *Man in the Age of Technology* (1980) uses "subjectivization"; see Peter Berger's introduction to the book for a discussion of the term in Gehlen's theory of modern institutions.

17. For a discussion of Taylor's methodology, see Craig Calhoun's (1991b) article. Calhoun criticizes Taylor for his neglect of the sociological factors that bear directly on his subject. Despite this criticism, Calhoun argues that Taylor's work is an excellent starting point for understanding the self as moral subject.

18. For a documentation and critical use of recent writings in modern history of emotions, see William Reddy's (2001) study whose principal research setting is revolutionary France and its sentimentalism in literature and philosophy. See also his (1997) *The Invisible Code: Honor and Sentiment in Post-Revolutionary France, 1815–1848*.

19. I would include here Max Scheler's *The Nature of Sympathy* ([1954] 1970) and his *Ressentiment* (1961), Georg Simmel's (1950) treatment of the social psychological implications of secrecy and betrayal and his essays on women and love (Oakes 1984), and Helen Merrell Lynd's (1958) now-classic work on the role of shame and its relationship to guilt. Harold

Bershady has provided for the English reader a valuable edited collection of Max Scheler's writings (1992) as well as an introduction to his work.

20. For commentaries on *The Civilizing Process*, see, in particular, Elias's (1968) appendix to the *The Civilizing Process* and Stephen Mennell's (1989, 188ff) discussion of this.

21. Taylor (1989, 493) cites a poem (of which I cite here only one line) by Wallace Stevens from his *Opus Posthumous*; for the full citation see Stephen Spender's *The Struggle of the Modern* (1963, 39).

CHAPTER 3

1. See C. Goldberg (1999). On a related topic see Thomas J. Scheff's account of his participation in a memorial to honor the dead Americans of the Iraq War, the poem "A Wake on the Pier" 2015), and essays #46 and #78 at www .soc.ucsb.edu/faculty/scheff; see also Scheff (2007).

2. "Eclipse of distance" is a theme elaborated by the late sociologist Daniel Bell in *The Cultural Contradictions of Capitalism* (1996). Regardless of their very different intents, it is a theme that resonates with Walter Benjamin's argument in "The Work of Art in the Age of Mechanical Reproduction" ([1950] 1969, 223): "Every day the urge grows stronger to get hold of an object at very close range." See also Andrew Robinson's article "Art, Aura, and Authenticity" (2013). The poet and cultural critic Aleš Debeljak (1998) uses Benjamin's idea of "aura" and the postmodern urge to move closer to address the arts in postmodernity; see chapter 5.

CHAPTER 4

1. See Mark Neocleous's *Fascism* (1997) and the collection *Fascism* (1995) edited by Roger Griffin, particularly Part IV. On nationalism, see *Nations and Nationalism* (2008) by Ernest Gellner and John Breuilly and *Nationalism* (1994) edited by J. Hutchinson and A. D. Smith.

2. In 1898, the year following her death, her autobiography, *Histoire d'une Ame*, was published (see Thérèse of Lisieux 1926). The extraordinary history of its distribution, translations, and popular success is documented by Gaucher ([1982] 1987) and others.

3. Now-classic studies of mass media and identity include the early studies by Altheide and Snow (1979), Joshua Meyrowitz (1985), and John Thompson (1995), who gave us some of the first terms for understanding how social relations are repositioned by mass media. Later works advance work and

theory on these issues: David Altheide (2014) shows us the effects through a study of the emotion of fear. Todd Gitlin's *Media Unlimited* (2002) is a work on the overwhelming environment of mass media. Catherine Wilson's highly original philosophical essay "Vicariousness and Authenticity" (2000) teaches us about the *experience* of technology today and how it points to an epistemology that breaks with the older one of "experience" and "proximity." See also Hal Foster's *Vision and Visuality* (1998).

4. I am using Thompson's (1995) terms from his theory of modern mass media and using recent examples of my own. His examples are often drawn from television and television broadcasting. In Meyrowitz (1985) the applications are most often drawn from television, too, but both studies anticipate the growing role of new technologies like the computer. I am indebted to Professor Paul Levinson at Fordham University for directing me to an excellent source for understanding media relations as "close." See Meyrowitz (2002) for a treatment of "media friends."

5. I am using and applying the concept invented by Daniel Bell (1996) to describe today's "eclipse of distance," as I did in chapter 3 (note 2).

6. "Only Connect." The full quote from E. M. Forster's novel *Howard's End*, (1910), chapter 22, is: "Only connect! That was the whole of her sermon. Only connect the prose and the passion, and both will be exalted, and human love will be seen at its height. Live in fragments no longer. Only connect, and the beast and the monk, robbed of the isolation that is life to either, will die." The short phrase "Only Connect!" is used as an imperative in today's mediatized world; it also points to the fact that digital connection is not only something technically possible, it is an *ethos* as well.

7. Charles Taylor concludes the chapter on "direct-access" with reflections on contemporary individualism and acknowledges his indebtedness to the work of sociologist Craig Calhoun, especially "Nationalism and Ethnicity" (1993).

8. My reading of others' works close to my topic tells me that my own ideas about public and collective emotions as experiences of *real emotion* and authenticity will probably not convince these scholars. Barbara Ehrenreich's *Dancing in the Streets: A History of Collective Joy* (2006) really challenged me to rethink much of what I write here, especially her palpable sense of the "loss" of collective joy from our world today. Lauren

Langman's (2012) argument about the carnivalesque features of postmodern life comes out of an important Marxist and Frankfurt School tradition
of thought about the inauthenticity of today's pleasure sites and carnivals. I
remain, for now, a stubborn opponent of social theories that teach us that
we are "false conscious," and I move with more ease and conviction with
theories of "human agency" that portray the remarkable human ability we
have to act even, and especially, in the face of overwhelming ideologies
(see, for example, Joas 1996).

References

Adorno, Theodor. *The Jargon of Authenticity*. New York: Routledge, [1964] 2007.

Alexander, Jeffrey C. *Positivism, Presuppositions, and Current Controversies.* Vol. 1 of *Theoretical Logic in Sociology*. Berkeley: University of California Press, 1982.

"Analytic Debates: Understanding the Relative Autonomy of Culture." In *Culture and Society*, edited by J. Alexander and S. Seidman, 1–27. New York: Cambridge, 1990.

The Meanings of Social Life: A Cultural Sociology. New York: Oxford University Press, 2003.

The Civil Sphere. New York: Oxford University Press, 2006.

The Performance of Politics: Obama's Victory and the Democratic Struggle for Power. New York: Oxford University Press, 2010.

Alexander, Jeffrey C., Bernhard Giesen, and Jason L. Mast. *Social Performance*. New York: Cambridge University Press, 2006.

Alexander, Jeffrey C., Ronald N. Jacobs, and Philip Smith. *The Oxford Companion to Cultural Sociology*. New York: Oxford University Press, 2012.

Alexander, Jeffrey C. and Jason L. Mast. "Introduction: Symbolic Action in Theory and Practice: The Cultural Pragmatics of Symbolic Action." In *Social Performance*, edited by J. C. Alexander, B. Giesen and J. L. Mast, 1–28. New York: Cambridge University Press, 2006.

Alexander, Jeffrey C. and Steven Seidman. *Culture and Society: Contemporary Debates*. New York: Cambridge, 1990.

Allan, Kenneth. "The Postmodern Self." *Quarterly Journal of Ideology* 20, no.1 and 2 (1997): 3–24.

Altheide, David L. *Media Edge: Media Logic and Social Reality*. New York: Peter Lang, 2014.

Altheide, David L. and Robert P. Snow. *Media Logic*. London: Sage, 1979.

Anderson, Benedict. *Imagined Communities*. Rev. ed. New York: Verso, [1983] 1991.

Appiah, Kwame Anthony and Henry Louis Gates, Jr. *Identities*. Chicago: University of Chicago Press, 1995.

Archer, Margaret S. *Culture and Agency: The Place of Culture in Social Theory*. New York: Cambridge University Press, 1988.

Ariès, Phillipe. *Centuries of Childhood: A Social History of Family Life*. New York: Vintage Books, 1962.

Aronowitz, Stanley. *The Politics of Identity: Class, Culture, Social Movements*. New York: Routledge, 1992.

Associated Press. "Area Firefighters to Attend Service for Fallen Hero." WHIO, March 26, 2015. www.whio.com/news/news/local/cincinnati-firefighter-falls-down-elevator-shaft/nkfmK/.

Association for the Study of Ethnicity. *Nations and Nationalism: Journal of the Association for the Study of Ethnicity and Nationalism* 1, part 1 (March 1995).

Averill, James R. "A Constructionist View of Emotion." In *Theories of Emotion*, edited by R. Plutchik and H. Kellerman, 305–39. New York: Basil Blackwell, 1980.

Anger and Aggression. New York: Springer-Verlag, 1982.

"The Acquisition of Emotions during Adulthood." In *The Social Construction of Emotion*, edited by R. Harre, 98–119. New York: Basil Blackwell, 1986.

Rules of Hope. New York: Springer-Verlag, 1990.

"Emotional Realism." *Cognition and Emotion* 10, no. 4 (1996): 425–35.

Averill, James R. and Elma P. Nunley. *Voyages of the Heart: Living an Emotionally Creative Life*. New York: Maxwell Macmillan International, 1992.

Ayres, B. Drummond. "After 10 Years of Tears, Memorials Keeps Healing." *New York Times*, November 11, 1992.

Baldwin, James. "The Discovery of What It Means to Be an American" originally appeared in *New York Times Book Review*, January 25, 1959.

Baldwin, John D. "Social Behaviorism on Emotions: Mead and Modern Behaviorism Compared." *Symbolic Interaction* 8, no. 2 (1985): 263–89.

Barbalet, J. M. *Emotion, Social Theory, and Social Structure: A Macrosociological Approach*. Cambridge, UK: Cambridge University Press, 1998.

Barthes, Roland. *Mythologies*. Translated by A. Lavers. New York: Hill and Wang, [1957] 1972.

Bauman, Zygmunt. "From Pilgrim to Tourist—Or a Short History of Identity." In *Questions of Cultural Identity*, edited by Stuart Hall and Paul du Gay, 18–36. London: Sage Publications, 1996.

Liquid Life. New York: Polity Press, 2005

Baumeister, Roy F. *Identity*. New York: Oxford, 1986.

"How the Self Became a Problem: A Psychological Review of Historical Research." *Journal of Personality and Social Psychology* 52, no.1 (1987a): 163–76.

"Identity, Self-Concept, and Self-Esteem." In *Handbook of Personality Psychology*, edited by Robert Hogan, John Johnson, and Stephen Briggs, 681–710. San Diego, CA: Academic Press, 1987b.

Meanings of Life. New York: Guilford, 1991.

Bell, Daniel. *The Winding Passage: Essays and Sociological Journeys.* New edition, with an introduction by Irving Louis Horowitz. New Brunswick, NJ: Transaction, [1980] 1991.

The Cultural Contradictions of Capitalism. 2nd ed. New York: Basic Books, 1996.

Benjamin, Walter. "The Work of Art in the Age of Mechanical Reproduction." In *Illuminations*, translated by H. Zohn and edited by H. Arendt, 217–52. New York: Schocken, [1950] 1969.

Benton, James S. "Self and Society in Popular Social Criticism: 1920–1980." *Symbolic Interaction* 16, no. 2 (1993): 145–70.

Berg, A. Scott. *Lindbergh.* New York: Putnam, 1998.

Berger, Peter L. *Invitation to Sociology.* Garden City, NY: Doubleday, 1963.

"Identity as a Problem in the Sociology of Knowledge." In *The Sociology of Knowledge*, edited by J. Curtis and J. Petras, 373–84. New York: Praeger, 1970.

"Toward a Sociological Understanding of Psychoanalysis." In *Facing Up to Modernity*, edited by P.L. Berger, 23–34. New York: Basic Books, 1977.

Berger, Peter L., Brigitte Berger, and Hansfried Kellner. *The Homeless Mind.* New York: Random House, 1973.

Berger, Peter L. and Thomas Luckmann. *The Social Construction of Reality.* Garden City, New York: Doubleday, 1966.

Berman, Marshall. *All That is Solid Melts into Air: The Experience of Modernity.* New York: Penguin, 1982.

"Why Modernism Still Matters." In *Modernity and Identity*, edited by Scott Lasch and Jonathan Friedman, 33–58. New York: Blackwell, 1992.

Blumer, Herbert. *Symbolic Interactionism.* Englewood Cliffs, NJ: Prentice Hall, 1969.

Bonnell, Victoria E. and Lynn Hunt, eds. *Beyond the Cultural Turn.* Berkeley: University of California Press, 1999.

Boorstin, Daniel J. *The Image: A Guide to Pseudo-events in America.* New York: Vintage, 1961.

Bourdieu, Pierre. *Outline of a Theory of Practice.* Cambridge, UK: Cambridge University Press, [1972] 1977.

Distinction: A Social Critique of the Judgement of Taste. London: Routledge, [1979] 1984.

boyd, dana. *It's Complicated: The Social Lives of Networked Teens.* New Haven, CT: Yale University Press, 2014.

Brady, J.V. "Toward a Behavioral Biology of Emotion." In *Emotions: Their Parameters and Measurement,* edited by L. Levi, 17–45. New York: Raven Press, 1975.

Braun, Jerome and Lauren Langman, eds. *Alienation and the Carnivalization of Society.* New York: Routledge, 2012.

Brennan, Teresa. *Exhausting Modernity.* New York: Routledge, 2000.

——— *The Transmission of Affect.* Ithaca, NY: Cornell University Press, 2004.

Bryant, Clifton D. *Handbook of Death and Dying.* 2 vols. Thousand Oaks, CA: Sage, 2003.

Burgett, Bruce and Glenn Hendler, eds. *Keywords for American Cultural Studies.* New York: New York University Press, 2007.

Burke, Kenneth. *Grammar of Motives.* New York: Prentice Hall, 1945.

——— *Philosophy of Literary Form.* 3rd ed. Berkeley: University of California Press, 1973.

Burckhardt, Jacob. *The Civilization of the Renaissance in Italy.* New York: The Modern Library, [1890] 1954.

Butterfield, Andrew. "Monuments and Memorials." *The New Republic* 3, (2003): 27–32.

Cahill, Spencer E. "Toward a Sociology of the Person." *Sociological Theory* 16, no. 2 (1997): 131–48.

Calhoun, Craig. "Community: Toward a Variable Conceptualization for Comparative Research." *Social History* 5, no. 1 (1980): 105–29.

——— "Populist Politics, Communications Media, and Large Scale Social Integration." *Sociological Theory* 6, no. 2 (1988): 219–41.

——— "Indirect Relationships and Imagined Communities: Large-Scale Integration and the Transformation of Everyday Life." In *Social Theory for a Changing Society,* edited by P. Bourdieu and J. Coleman, 9–36. Boulder, CO: Westview Press. 1991a.

——— "Morality, Identity, and Historical Explanation: Charles Taylor on *The Sources of the Self. Sociological Theory* 9, no.2 (1991b): 232–63.

——— "The Infrastructure of Modernity: Indirect Social Relationships, Information Technology, and Social Integration." In *Social Change and Modernity,* edited by Hans Haferkamp and Neil J. Smelser, 205–36. Berkley: University of California Press, 1992.

——— "Nationalism and Civil Society: Democracy, Diversity, and Self-Determination." *International Sociology* 8, no. 4 (1993a): 387–411.

"Nationalism and Ethnicity." *Annual Review of Sociology* 19, no. 9 (1993b): 211–39.

Social Theory and the Politics of Identity. Cambridge, MA: Blackwell, 1994.

Nationalism. Minneapolis: University of Minnesota Press, 1997.

"The Problematic Public: Revisiting Dewey, Arendt, and Habermas." Presentation at the University of Michigan, April 11, 2013. www .tannerlectures.utah.edu.

Canetti, Elias. *Crowds and Power.* New York: Seabury Press, 1962.

Carter, Holland. "The 9/11 Story Told at Bedrock, Powerful as a Punch to the Gut," Art and Design. *New York Times,* May 14, 2014. www.nytimes.com/2014/ 05/14/arts/design/sept-11-memorial-museum-at-ground-zero-prepares-for-opening.html?emc=eta1.

Cerulo, Karen. "Identity Construction: New Issues, New Directions." *Annual Review of Sociology* 23, (1997): 385–409.

Culture in Mind: Toward a Sociology of Culture and Cognition. New York: Routledge, 2002.

Clark, Candace. *Misery and Company: Sympathy in Everyday Life.* Chicago: University of Chicago Press, 1997.

Chodorow, Nancy J. *The Power of Feelings.* New Haven, CT: Yale University Press, 1999.

Clifford, James. *The Predicament of Culture.* Cambridge, MA: Harvard University Press, 1988.

Collins, Randall. "On the Microfoundations of Macrosociology." *American Journal of Sociology* 86, no. 5 (1981): 984–1014.

Interaction Ritual Chains. Princeton, NJ: Princeton University Press, 2004.

Cooley, C.H. *Social Organization: A Study of the Larger Mind.* New York: Shocken Books, [1909] 1962.

Coulter-Smith, Graham. *Deconstructing Installation Art: Fine Art and Media Art, 1986–2006.* First published by CASIAD, Southampton Solent University, 2006; accessed January 4, 2016. www.installationart.net.

Crane, Diana. *The Sociology of Culture: Emerging Theoretical Perspectives.* London: Blackwell, 1994.

Crapanzano, Vincent. *Hermes' Dilemma and Hamlet's Desire.* Cambridge, MA: Harvard University Press, 1992.

Darnton, Robert. *Mesmerism.* New York: Schocken, 1968.

Debeljak, Aleš. *Reluctant Modernity: The Institution of Art and Its Historical Forms.* New York: Rowman and Littlefield, 1998.

De Grazia, Sabastian. *Of Time, Work, and Leisure.* New York: Vintage Books, 1962.

DeJean, Joan. *Ancients against Moderns: Culture Wars and the Making of a Fin de Siècle.* Chicago: University of Chicago Press, 1997.

Denzin, Norman K. *On Understanding Emotion.* San Francisco: Jossey-Bass, 1984.

Symbolic Interaction and Cultural Studies. Cambridge, MA: Blackwell, 1992.

Derne, Steve. "Structural Realities, Persistent Dilemmas, and the Construction of Emotional Paradigms: Love in Three Cultures," In *Social Perspectives on Emotion*, vol. 2, edited by William M. Wentworth and John Ryan, 281–308. Greenwich, CT: JAI Press, 1994.

de Sousa, Ronald. *The Rationality of Emotion.* Cambridge, MA: MIT Press, 1987.

Dewey, John. *Logic.* New York: Henry Holt, 1936.

Doveling, Katrin, C. von Scheve, and E. A. Konijn, *The Routledge Handbook of Emotions and Mass Media.* New York: Routledge, 2011.

DuBois, W. E. B. *The Souls of Black Folk.* New York: Dover, [1903]1994.

Dunning, Eric. *Sport Matters: Sociological Studies of Sport, Violence, and Civilization.* London: Routledge, 1999.

Durkheim, Emile. *The Division of Labor in Society.* New edition, with an introduction by Lewis Coser. Translated by W. D. Halls. New York: Free Press, [1893] 1984.

Eagleton, Terry. *The Idea of Culture.* Oxford, UK: Blackwell, 2000.

Ehrenreich, Barbara. *Dancing in the Streets: A History of Collective Joy.* New York: Henry Holt., 2006.

Ekman, Paul, ed. *Emotion in the Human Face*, 2nd ed. Cambridge, UK: Cambridge University Press, 1982.

Eksteins, Modris. *Rites of Spring: The Great War and the Birth of the Modern Age.* New York: Doubleday/Anchor, 1989.

Elias, Norbert. *The Civilizing Process: Sociogenetic and Psychogenetic Investigations.* Rev. ed. Edited by E. Dunning, J. Goudsblom, and S. Mennell. Translated by E. Jephcott, with some notes and corrections by the author. Oxford, UK: Blackwell, [1939] 2000.

The Germans: Power Struggles and the Development of Habitus in the Nineteenth and Twentieth Centuries. Translated from the German and with a preface by Eric Dunning and Stephen Mennell. New York: Columbia University Press, 1996.

The Society of Individuals. Edited by M. Schöter. Translated by E. Jephcott. London: Continuum, 2001.

Elias, Norbert and Eric Dunning. *Quest for Excitement.* New York: Blackwell, 1986.

Elliot, Anthony. *Concepts of the Self.* 1st ed. London: Polity, 2001.

Elliot, Anthony and Charles Lemert. *The New Individualism: The Emotional Costs of Globalization*. London: Routledge, 2006.

Emerson, E. W. and W. Emerson, eds. *From the Journals of Ralph Waldo Emerson*. 10 vols. Boston: Houghton Mifflin, 1909–14.

Engdahl, Emma. *A Theory of the Emotional Self: From the Standpoint of a Neo-Meadian*. Örebro Studies in Sociology. Örebro, Sweden: Örebro University, 2004.

Erikson, Erik H. *Childhood and Society*. 2nd ed. New York: Norton, 1963.

Identity: Youth and Crisis. New York: Norton, 1968.

Farberman, Harvey A. "Mannheim, Cooley, and Mead: Toward a Social Theory of Mentality." In *Towards the Sociology of Knowledge: Origin and Development of a Sociological Thought Style*, edited by G. Remmling, 1–13. New York: Humanities Press, 1970.

Fernandez, Manny. "Shoulder to Shoulder, In Grief." *New York Times*. March 13, 2007a. www.nytimes.com/2007/03/13/nyregion/13scene.html.

"In the Bronx, an Early Lesson on Goodbye." *New York Times*. March 31, 2007b. www.nytimes.com/2007/03/31/nyregion/31school.html?pagewanted=print&_r=0.

Fernandez, Manny and Timothy Williams. "Collective Grief after a Blaze Claims Eight of a Bronx Neighborhood's Many Children." *New York Times*. March 9th, 2007. www.nytimes.com/2007/03/09/nyregion/09neighbor hood.html.

Foster, Hal. *Vision and Visuality: Discussions in Contemporary Culture (Book # 2)*. New York: New Press. 1998.

Foucault, Michel. "Prison Talk." Translated by C. Gordon. *Radical Philosophy*, no. 16 (Spring 1977).

"What Is Enlightenment?" In *The Foucault Reader*, edited by P. Rabinow, 32–50. New York: Pantheon, 1984.

Foucault, Michel, Luther H. Martin, Huck Gutman, and Patrick H. Hutton. *Technologies of the Self: A Seminar with Michel Foucault*. Amherst: University of Massachusetts Press, 1988.

Franks, David D. "Introduction to the Special Issue on the Sociology of Emotions. *Symbolic Interaction* 8, no. 2 (1985): 161–70.

"Mutual Interests, Different Lenses: Current Neuroscience and Symbolic Interaction." *Symbolic Interaction* 26, no.4 (2003): 613–30.

Neurosociology: The Nexus between Neuroscience and Social Psychology. New York: Springer Press, 2010.

Franks, David D. and E. Doyle McCarthy. *The Sociology of Emotions: Original Essays and Research Papers*. Greenwich, CT: JAI Press, 1989.

Franks, David, and Thomas Smith. "Mind, Brain, and Society: Toward a Neurosociology of Emotion" *Social Perspectives on Emotion Interaction* 5 (1997).

Franks, David, and Jonathan H. Turner. *The Handbook of Social Psychology.* New York: Springer, 2012.

The Handbook of Neurosociology. New York: Springer, 2013.

Freud, Sigmund. *The Ego and the Id.* New York: Norton, [1923] 1960.

Frevert, Ute. "Defining Emotions: Concepts and Debates over Three Centuries." In *Emotional Lexicons: Continuity and Change in the Vocabulary of Feeling, 1700–2000,* edited by Ute Frevert, Monique Scheer, Pascal Eitler, Anne Schmidt, Bettina Hitzer, Christian Bailey, Benno Gammerl, Nina Verheyen, and Margrit Pernau, 1–31. Oxford, UK: Oxford University Press, 2014.

Frevert, Ute, Monique Scheer, Pascal Eitler, Anne Schmidt, Bettina Hitzer, Christian Bailey, Benno Gammerl, Nina Verheyen, and Margrit Pernau. *Emotional Lexicons: Continuity and Change in the Vocabulary of Feeling, 1700–2000.* Oxford, UK: Oxford University Press, 2014.

Friedrichs, Robert W. *A Sociology of Sociology.* New York: Free Press, 1970.

Frijda, Nico H. *The Emotions.* New York: Cambridge University Press, 1986.

Frijda, Nico H., Anthony S. R. Manstead, and Sacha Bem. *Emotions and Beliefs: How Feelings Influence Thoughts.* New York: Cambridge University Press, 2000.

Gabler, Neal. *Life the Movie: How Entertainment Conquered Reality.* New York: Knopf, 1998.

Gallant, Thomas. "Long Time Coming, Long Time Gone: The Past, Present and Future of Social History." *Historeim* (2012): 9–12.

Garber, Marjorie, Jann Matlock, and Rebecca L. Walkowitz. *Media Spectacles.* New York: Routledge, 1993.

Gaucher, Guy. *The Story of a Life: St Thérèsa of Lisieux.* New York: Harper Collins, [1982] 1987.

Gay, Peter. *The Enlightenment: The Science of Freedom.* Vol. 2. New York: Knopf, 1969.

Education of the Senses. Vol. 1 of *The Bourgeois Experience: Victoria to Freud.* New York: Oxford University Press, 1984.

The Tender Passion. Vol. 2 of *The Bourgeois Experience: Victoria to Freud.* New York: Oxford University Press, 1986.

The Cultivation of Hatred. Vol. 3 of *The Bourgeois Experience: Victoria to Freud.* New York: Norton, 1993.

The Naked Heart. New York: Norton, 1995.

Gecas, Viktor. "The Self Concept." *Annual Review of Sociology.* 8 (1982): 1–13.

Geertz, Clifford. *The Interpretation of Cultures.* New York: Basic Books, [1973] 2000a.

———. "'From the Native's Point of View': On the Nature of Anthropological Understanding." *Bulletin of the American Academy of Arts and Sciences* 28 (1974).

———. *Local Knowledge.* New York: Basic Books, [1983] 2000b.

———. *After the Fact.* Cambridge, MA: Harvard University Press. 1995.

———. "Interview with Clifford Geertz." In *Ethnographica Moralia: Experiments in Interpretive Anthropology,* edited by Neni Panourgia and George E. Marcus, 15–28. New York: Fordham University Press, 2008.

Geertz, Hildred. "The Vocabulary of Emotion: A Study of Javanese Socialization." *Psychiatry* 22 (1959): 225–37.

Gehlen. Arnold. *Man in the Age of Technology.* New York: Columbia University Press, 1980.

Gellner, Ernest, and John Breuilly. *Nations and Nationalism.* Published by the Journal of the Association for the Study of Ethnicity and Nationalism, 2008.

Gergen, Kenneth J. "The Social Constructionist Movement in Modern Psychology." *The American Psychologist* 40, no.3 (1985): 266–75.

———. *The Saturated Self.* New York: Basic Books, 1991.

———. *Social Construction in Context.* Thousand Oaks, CA: Sage, 2001.

———. *An Invitation to Social Construction.* 2nd ed. Thousand Oaks, CA: Sage, 2009.

Gergen, Kenneth J. and Keith E. Davis. *The Social Construction of the Person.* New York: Springer, 1985.

Gergen, Mary M., and Kenneth J. Gergen. "What Is This Thing Called Love? Emotional Scenarios in Historical Perspective." *Journal of Narrative and Life History* 5, no. 3 (1995): 221–37.

Giddens, Anthony. *Modernity and Self-Identity.* Stanford, CA: Stanford University Press, 1991.

———. *Runaway World: How Globalization Is Shaping Our Lives.* New York: Routledge, 2000.

Giesen, Bernhard. "Performing the Sacred." In *Social Performance,* edited by J. Alexander, B. Giesen, and J. L. Mast, 326–367. New York: Cambridge University Press, 2006.

Gitlin, Todd. *Media Unlimited.* New York: Henry Holt, 2002.

Glassner, Barry. *The Culture of Fear: Why Americans Are Afraid of the Wrong Things.* New York: Basic Books, 1999.

Glazer, Nathan. "Monuments in an Age without Heroes," *The Public Interest* (September 1996): 22–39.

Gleason, Philip. "Identifying Identity: A Semantic History." *The Journal of American History* (1983): 910–31.

Goffman, Erving. *The Presentation of Self in Everyday Life.* Garden City, NY: Doubleday Anchor, 1959.

Encounters: Two Studies in the Sociology of Interaction. Indianapolis: Bobs-Merrill, 1961.

Interaction Ritual: Essays on Face-to-Face Behavior. New York: Anchor, 1967.

Gender Advertisements. Introduction by Vivian Gornick. New York: Harper and Row, 1976.

"The Interaction Order: American Sociological Association, 1982 Presidential Address." *American Sociological Review* (1983): 1–17.

Goldberg, Carey. "Feelings of Deep Grief, Even When Their Cause Surpasses Understanding." *New York Times*, July 23, 1999.

Goldberg, Ken. *The Robot in the Garden: Telerobotics and Telepistemology in the Age of Internet.* Cambridge, MA: MIT Press, 2000.

Goldberger, Paul. "Down at the Mall." *New Yorker*, May 31, 2004a. www .newyorker.com/magazine/2004/05/31/down-at-the-mall.

Up From Zero: Politics, Architecture, and the Rebuilding of New York. New York: Random House, 2004b.

Building Up and Tearing Down: Reflections on the Age of Architecture. New York: The Monacelli Press, Random House, 2009.

Goleman, Daniel. *Emotional Intelligence.* New York: Bantam Books, 1995.

Goodwin, Jeff, James M. Jasper, and Francesca Polletta. *Passionate Politics: Emotions and Social Movements.* Chicago: University of Chicago Press, 2001.

Gordon, Steven L. "The Sociology of Sentiments and Emotions." In *Social Psychology: Sociological*, edited by Rosenberg, Morris and Ralph H. Turner, 261–78. New York: Basic Books, 1981.

"Institutional and Impulsive Orientations in Selectively Appropriating Emotions to Self." In *The Sociology of Emotions*, edited by David D. Franks and E. Doyle McCarthy, 115–35. Greenwich, CT: JAI Press, 1989.

"Social Structural Effects on Emotions." In *Research Agendas in the Sociology of Emotions*, edited by Theodore D. Kemper, 145–79. SUNY Press, 1990.

Gramsci, Antonio. *Selections from the Prison Notebooks of Antonio Gramsci.* Edited and translated by Geoffrey Nowell-Smith and Quintin Hoare. London: Lawrence and Wishart, 1971.

Graumann, Carl F. and Kenneth J. Gergen, *Historical Dimensions of Psychological Discourse*. New York: Cambridge University Press, 1996.

Greenberg, Michael. "The NY Police vs. the Mayor." *New York Review of Books*, February 5, 2015. www.nybooks.com/articles/2015/02/05/ny-police-vs-mayor/.

Greenblatt, Stephen. *Renaissance Self-Fashioning. From More to Shakespeare*. Chicago. University of Chicago Press, 1980.

Greenspan, Jesse. "Six Things You May Not Know about the Vietnam Veterans Memorial." History.com, November 13, 2012. http://www.history.com/news/6-things-you-may-not-know-about-the-vietnam-veterans-memorial.

Gregoire, Carolyn. "How Emotionally Intelligent Are You? Here's How to Tell." *The Huffington Post*, December 5, 2013; last modified January 23, 2014. www.huffingtonpost.com/2013/12/05/are-you-emotionally-intel_n_4371920.html.

Griffin, Roger, ed. *Fascism*. Oxford: UK: Oxford University Press, 1995.

Gross, Edward. "The Social Construction of Historical Events through Public Dramas." *Symbolic Interaction*, 9 (1986): 179–200.

Gross, Jane. "Small Gestures of Grief for a Young Man Larger than Life." *New York Times*, July 22, 1999.

Gulbenkian Commission. *Open the Social Sciences: Report of the Gulbenkian Commission on the Restructuring of the Social Sciences*. Stanford, CA: Stanford University Press, 1996.

Guttman, Allen. *Sports: The First Five Millennia*. Boston, MA: University of Massachusetts Press, 2004.

Hacking, Ian. *The Social Construction of What?* Cambridge: Harvard University Press, 1999.

Hall, Stuart. *Culture, Media, Language: Working Papers in Cultural Studies, 1972–1979*. London: Hutchinson, 1980.

"Who Needs Identity?" In *Questions of Cultural Identity*, edited by S. Hall and Paul du Gay, 1–17. London: Sage, 1996.

Hanin, Yuri L. *Emotions in Sport*. Champaign, IL: Human Kenetics, 1999.

Harland, Richard. *Superstructuralism: The Philosophy of Structuralism and Post-Structuralism*. London: Mathuen, 1987.

Harré, Rom. *The Social Construction of Emotions*. London: Basil Blackwell, 1986.

Physical Being: A Theory for a Corporeal Psychology. Oxford: Basil Blackwell, 1991.

Harré, Rom, and W. Gerrod Parrott, eds. *The Emotions: Social, Cultural, and Biological Dimension*. Thousand Oaks, CA: Sage, 1986.

Harris, Ruth. *Lourdes: Body and Spirit in the Secular Age.* New York: Penguin, 1999

Harris, Scott R. *An Invitation to the Sociology of Emotions.* New York: Routledge, 2015.

Harvard Design Magazine. "Constructions of Memory: On Monuments Old and New." Special issue, no. 9 (Fall 1999). www.harvarddesignmagazine.org./issues/9.

Harvey, Daina Cheyenne. "A Quiet Suffering: Some Notes on the Sociology of Suffering." *Sociological Forum* 27, no.2 (2012): 527–34.

Hedgehog Review. "Identity." Special issue, vol. 1 (Fall 1999). "Celebrity Culture." Special issue, vol. 7 (Spring. 2005).

Heise, David. "Social Action as the Control of Affect." 22 (1977): 163–77.

Heller, Thomas C., Morton Sosna, and David Wellbery. *Reconstructing Individualism: Autonomy, Individuality, and the Self in Western Thought.* Stanford, CA: Stanford University Press, 1986.

Hewitt, John P. *Dilemmas of the American Self.* Philadelphia: Temple University Press, 1989.

    The Myth of Self-Esteem: Finding Happiness and Solving Problems in America. New York: St. Martin's, 1998.

Hickey, McGee. "Bruce Springsteen Fans Reminisce on 40th Birthday of 'Born to Run'." Pix11.com, August 10, 2015. http://pix11.com/2015/08/25/bruce-springsteen-fans-reminisce-on-40th-birthday-of-born-to-run/.

Higgins, John. *The Raymond Williams Reader.* Oxford, UK: Blackwell, 2001.

Hobsbawm, Eric. *Nations and Nationalism since 1780.* Cambridge, UK: Canto, 1990.

    The Age of Extremes: A History of the World, 1914–1991. London: Abacus, 1994.

Hochschild, Arlie Russell. "Emotion Work, Feeling Rules, and Social Structure." *American Journal of Sociology* 35 (1979): 551–73.

    The Managed Heart: Commercialization of Human Feeling. Berkeley, CA: University of California Press, 1983.

Hollinger, David A, "The Disciplines and the Identity Debates, 1970–1995." *Daedalus* 126, no. 1, (Winter 1997): 333–51.

Holstein, James A. and Jaber F. Gubrium. *The Self We Live By Narrative Identity in a Postmodern World.* New York: Oxford University Press, 2000.

Howard, Judith A. "Social Psychology of Identities," *Annual Review of Sociology.* 26 (2000): 367–93.

Howe, Irving. *The Idea of the Modern in Literature and the Arts.* New York: Horizon, 1967.

Hughes, H. Stuart. *Consciousness and Society: The Reorientation of European Social Thought, 1890–1930*. New York: Knopf, 1958.

Hunt, Lynn. *The New Social History*. Berkeley: University of California Press, 1989.

Hutchinson, J. and A. D. Smith, eds. *Nationalism*. New York: Oxford, 1994.

Huyssen, Andreas. *Twilight Memories*. New York: Routledge, 1995.

Ibrahim, Yasmin. "Distant Suffering and Postmodern Subjectivity: The Communal Politics of Pity." *Nebula* (June 2010): 122–35.

Illouz, Eva. *Consuming the Romantic Utopia: Love and the Cultural Contradictions of Capitalism*. Berkeley: University of California Press, 1997.

    Oprah Winfrey and the Glamour of Misery: An Essay on Popular Culture. New York: Columbia University Press, 2003.

    Cold Intimacies. Cambridge, UK: Polity, 2007.

    Saving the Modern Soul. Berkeley: University of California Press, 2008.

    Why Love Hurts. Cambridge, UK: Polity, 2012.

Imber, Jonathan B. *Therapeutic Culture: Triumph and Defeat*. New Brunswick, NJ: Transaction, 2004.

Inkeles, Alex, and Daniel J. Levinson. "National Character: The Study of Modal Personality and Sociocultural Systems." *The Handbook of Social Psychology* 4 (1969): 418–506.

"It's Only a Paper Moon." A popular song written by Harold Arlen with lyrics by E.Y. Harburg and Billy Rose (1933). YouTube audio, 2:37, from a vocal performance by Ella Fitzgerald with the Delta Rhythm Boys. Posted on May 20, 2016. www.youtube.com/watch?v=ndxAZfJxfy8.

Janiskee, Bob. "By the Numbers: Vietnam Veterans Memorial." NationalParksTraveler.com, May 31, 2010. www.nationalparkstraveler.com.

Jarvie, Grant and Joseph Maguire. *Sport and Leisure in Social Thought*. London: Routledge, 1994.

Jasper, James. *Restless Nation: Starting Over in America*. Chicago: University of Chicago Press, 2000.

Johnson-Laird, N. and Keith Oatley. "The Language of Emotions: An Analysis of a Semantic Field." *Cognition and Emotion* 3, no. 2 (1989): 81–123.

Joas, Hans. *The Creativity of Action*. Chicago: University of Chicago Press, 1996.

Jungk, Peter S. *Franz Werfel: A Life*. New York: Grove Weidenfeld, 1987.

Kane, Anne. "Theorizing Meaning Construction in Social Movements," *Sociological Theory* 15 (1997): 249–76.

    "Finding Emotion in Social Movement Processes: Irish Land Movement Metaphors and Narratives." *Passionate Politics: Emotions and Social Movements* (2001): 251–66.

Katz, Jack. *How Emotions Work*. Chicago: University of Chicago Press, 1999.

Kaya, Ciğdem and Burcu Yağiz. "Appropriation in Souvenir Design and Production: A Study in Museum Shops." *ITU Journal of the Faculty of Architecture* 12 (March 2015): 127–46.

Kedourie, Elie. "Nationalism and Self-Determination." In *Nationalism*, edited by J. Hutchinson and A. D. Smith, 49–55. Oxford, UK: Oxford University Press, [1960] 1994.

Kellner, Douglas. "Media Communications vs. Cultural Studies: Overcoming the Divide." *Communication Theory* 5, no.2 (1995): 162–77.

Media Culture: Cultural Studies, Identity, and Politics between the Modern and the Post-Modern. London: Routledge, 2003a.

Media Spectacle. London: Routledge, 2003b.

Kemper, Theodore D. *A Social Interactional Theory of Emotions*. New York: John Wiley, 1978.

"How Many Emotions Are There? Wedding the Social and Automatic Components." *American Journal of Sociology* 93 (1987): 263–89.

ed. *Research Agendas in the Sociology of Emotions*. Albany: State University of New York Press, 1990.

Status, Power, and Ritual: A Relational Reading of Durkheim, Goffman, and Collins. Burlington, VT: Ashgate, 2011.

Kimmelman, Michael. "Out of Minimalism, Monuments to Memory." *New York Times*, January 13, 2002.

"The Craving for Public Squares." *New York Review of Books*, April 7, 2016. www.nybooks.com/articles/2016/04/07/craving-for-public-squares/.

Klein, Herbert S. "The Old Social History and the New Social Sciences," *Journal of Social History* 39, no. 3 (Spring 2006): 935–44.

Kleinman, Arthur and Joan Kleinman. 1997. "The Appeal of Suffering; The Dismay of Images: Cultural Appropriations of Suffering in Our Times." In *Social Suffering*, edited by A. Kleinman, V. Das, and N. Lock, 1–23. Berkeley: University of California Press, 1997.

Kleinman, Arthur, Veena Das, and Margaret Lock. *Social Suffering*. Berkeley: University of California Press, 1997.

Kleinman, Sherryl. *Opposing Ambitions: Gender and Identity in an Alternative Organization*. Chicago: University of Chicago Press, 1996.

Knox, R. A. *Enthusiasm: A Chapter in the History of Religion*. Oxford, UK: Clarendon, 1950.

Kracauer, Siegfried. *The Mass Ornament: Weimar Essays*. Cambridge, MA: Harvard University Press, 1995.

Krakauer, Jon. *Into Thin Air: A Personal Account of the Mount Everest Disaster.* New York: Anchor/Doubleday, 1997.

Kropp, Goran with David Lagercrantz. *Ultimate High: My Everest Odyssey.* New York: Discovery Books, 1997.

Kuhn, Thomas S. *The Structure of Scientific Revolutions.* 2nd ed. Chicago: University of Chicago Press, [1962] 1970.

Langman, Lauren. "Alienation, Entrapment, and Inauthenticity: Carnival to the Rescue." In *Alienation and the Carnivalization of Society,* edited by J. Braun and L. Langman, 53–73. New York: Routledge, 2012.

Laqueur, Walter. *The Terrible Secret: Suppression of the Truth about Hitler's "Final Solution."* Rev. ed. New York: Owls Books, [1980]1998.

Lasch, Christopher. *The Culture of Narcissism.* New York: Norton, 1978.

Lash, Scott and Jonathan Friedman. *Modernity and Identity.* Blackwell, 1992.

Le Bon, Gustave. *The Crowd.* 2nd ed. Marietta, GA: Larking Corp, 1895.

Lever, Janet. *Soccer Madness.* Chicago: University of Chicago Press, 1983.

Lévi-Strauss, Claude. *Totemism.* Translated by R. Needham. New York: Penguin, [1962] 1969.

　The Savage Mind. Chicago: University of Chicago Press, 1966.

Lin, Maya. "Untitled Statements." In *Contemporary Art: A Sourcebook of Artists' Writings,* edited by Kristine Stiles and Howard Setz, 524–25. Berkeley: University of California Press, 1996.

　"A Strong Clear Vision." A documentary film, directed by Freida Lee Mock. [1994] Released November 10, 1998.

　"Making the Monument." *New York Review of Books* 47, no. 17 (November 2, 2000).

　"Monumental Achievement. Our 2002 Profile of Architect Maya Lin That Marked the 20th Year of the Vietnam Memorial." Edited by Robert F. Howe. *Smithsonian,* November 1, 2002. www.Smithsonian.com.

Lin, Maya, Michael Brenson, William L. Fox, and Paul Goldberger. *Topologies.* New York: Rizzoli, 2015.

"Lindbergh's Atlantic Flight – Arrival at Le Bourget in Paris – Arrival at Croydon 1927." YouTube video, 5:00. Posted on April 13, 2014. https://www.youtube.com/watch?v=ubvWu2gXzZs.

Lincoln, Yvonna S., and Egon G. Guba. *The Constructivist Credo.* Walnut Creek, CA: Left Coast Press, 2013.

Linenthal, Edward. T. *Sacred Ground: Americans and their Battlefields.* 2nd ed. Champaign: University of Illinois Press, 1993.

　Preserving Memory: The Struggle to Create America's Holocaust Museum. New York: Columbia University Press, 1995.

The Unfinished Bombing. New York: Oxford University Press, 2001.

Lofland, Lyn H. "The Social Shaping of Emotion: The Case of Grief." *Symbolic Interaction.* (1985): 171–90.

Lowney, Kathleen S. *Baring Our Souls.* Hawthorne, NY: Aldine de Gruyter, 1999.

Luhmann, Niklas. "The Individuality of the Individual: Historical Meanings and Contemporary Problem." In *Reconstructing Individualism: Autonomy, Individuality, and the Self in Western Thought,* edited by Thomas C. Heller, Morton Sosna, and David Wellbery, 313–28. Stanford, CA: Stanford University Press, 1986.

Love as Passion: The Codification of Intimacy. Translated by J. Gaines and D.L. Jones. Stanford, CA: Stanford University Press, 1998.

The Reality of Mass Media. Translated by Kathleen Cross. Stanford, CA: Stanford University Press, 2000.

Lukes, Steven. *Individualism.* New York: Harper and Row, 1973.

Lupton, Deborah. *The Emotional Self.* London: Sage, 1988.

Lutz, Catherine A. *Unnatural Emotions.* Chicago: University of Chicago Press, 1988.

Lutz, Catherine A. and Lila Abu-Lughod. *Language and the Politics of Emotion.* New York: Cambridge University Press, 1990.

Lynd, Helen Merrell. *On Shame and the Search for Identity.* New York: Harcourt Brace, 1958.

Lyng, Stephen. "Edgework: A Social Psychological Analysis of Voluntary Risk Taking." *American Journal of Sociology* 95, no.4 (1990): 851–86.

Lyng, Stephen and David D. Franks. *Sociology and the Real World.* London: Rowman and Littlefield, 2002.

MacCannell, Dean. "Commemorative Essay: Erving Goffman (1922–1982)." *Semiotica.* 45 (1990): 1–33.

MacIntyre, Alasdair. *After Virtue.* Notre Dame, IN: University of Notre Dame Press, 1983.

Maguire, Joseph. *Global Sport: Identities, Societies, Civilizations.* Cambridge, UK: Polity Press, 1999.

Mannheim, Karl. "Historicism." In *Essays on the Sociology of Knowledge,* edited by Paul Kecskemeti, 84–133. London: Routledge and Kegan Paul, [1924] 1952.

Manstead, A. S., N. Frijda, and A. Fischer. *Feelings and Emotions.* New York: Cambridge University Press, 2004.

Marcus, G. E., and M. J. Fischer. *Anthropology as Cultural Critique: An Experimental Moment in the Human Sciences.* Chicago: University of Chicago Press, 1986.

Margolis, Diane Rothbard. *The Fabric of Self: A Theory of Ethics and Emotions.* New Haven, CT: Yale University Press, 1998.

Martin, Emily. *Flexible Bodies. Tracking Immunity in American Culture from the Days of Polio to the Age of AIDS.* Boston: Beacon Press, 1994.

McCall, George J. and J. L. Simmons. *Identities and Interactions.* New York: Free Press, 1966.

McCarthy, E. Doyle. "Emotions are Social Things: An Essay in the Sociology of Emotions." In *The Sociology of Emotions,* edited by David D. Franks and E. Doyle McCarthy, 51–72. Greenwich, CT: JAI Press, 1989a.

"The Interactionist Theory of Mind: A Sociology of Social Objects." *Studies in Symbolic Interaction* 10, (1989b): 79–86.

"The Social Construction of Emotions: New Directions from Culture Theory." In *Social Perspectives on Emotion,* vol. 2, edited by William M. Wentworth and John Ryan, 267–79. Greenwich, CT: JAI Press, 1994.

Knowledge as Culture: The New Sociology of Knowledge. New York: Routledge, 1996.

"Emotions: Senses of the Modern Self." Special Issue on *Sociologie Der Sinne* [Sociology of the Senses], *Österreichische Zeitschrift Für Soziologie* [Austrian Journal of Sociology] 27, no. 2 (2002): 30–49.

"Public Displays of Emotion Today: Memorializing Death and Disaster." Presentation at Columbia University, Seminar on Contents and Methods, February 14, 2007.

"Emotional Performances as Dramas of Authenticity." In *Authenticity in Culture, Self, and Society,* edited by Phillip Vannini and Patrick Williams, 241–55. London: Ashgate, 2009.

McClay, Wilfred M. *The Masterless: Self and Society in Modern America.* Chapel Hill: The University of North Carolina Press, 1994.

McGee, Micki. *Self-Help, Inc.: Makeover Culture in American Life.* New York: Oxford University Press, 2005.

McLuhan, Marshall. *Understanding Media: The Extensions of Man.* Cambridge, MA: MIT Press, [1964] 1994.

McPhail, Clark. *The Myth of the Maddening Crowd.* New York: Aldine de Gruyter, 1991.

Mead, George Herbert. *Mind, Self, and Society.* Chicago, IL: University of Chicago Press, 1934.

Mennell, Stephen. *Norbert Elias, Civilisation, and the Human Self-Image.* Oxford, UK: Blackwell, 1989.

Meštrović, Stjepan G. *Postemotional Society.* Thousand Oaks, CA: Sage, 1997.

Meyer, John. "Myths of Socialization and Personality." In *Reconstructing Individualism: Autonomy, Individuality, and the Self in Western Thought*, edited by Thomas C. Heller, 208–221. Stanford, CA: Stanford University Press, 1986.

Meyrowitz, Joshua. *No Sense of Place*. New York: Oxford University Press, 1985.
"The Majority Cult: Love and Grief for Media Friends." In *Les cultes médiatiques: Culture fan et oeuvres cultes*, edited by Philippe Le Guem, 133–62. Rennes: Presses Universitaires de Rennes, 2002.

Mitchell, Richard. *Mountain Experience: The Psychology and Sociology of Adventure*. Chicago: University of Chicago Press, 1983.

Mudimbe, V.Y., ed. *Open the Social Sciences: Report of the Gulbenkian Commission on the Restructuring of the Social Sciences*. Stanford, CA: Stanford University Press, 1996.

Muggeridge, Malcolm. *Muggeridge through the Microphone: BBC Radio and Television*. London: British Broadcasting Corporation, 1967.

Mukerji, Chandra. "The Search for Cultural Authenticity." *Culture*, Newsletter of the Sociology of Culture Section of the American Sociological Association 21, no.3 (2007): 1–2.

Mukerji, C. and M. Schudson. *Rethinking Popular Culture*. Berkeley: University of California Press, 1991.

Mumford, Lewis. *The Culture of Cities*." New York: Harcourt Brace, 1938.

Neocleous, Mark. *Fascism*. Minneapolis: University of Minnesota, 1997.

Noveck, Jocelyn. "On First U.S. Visit, Pope's Appeal Transcends Religion, Age, Politics." *New York Channel 4*, September 26, 2015. www.nbcnewyork .com/news/local/NYC-Pope-Francis-Transcends-Religion-Age-Politics-Ca ptivates-United-States-329647541.html.

Oakes, Guy. Introduction to and translation of *Georg Simmel: On Women, Sexuality, and Love*. New Haven, CT: Yale University Press, 1984.
Introduction to and translation of *Political Romanticism* by Carl Schmitt. Cambridge, MA: MIT Press, 1986.
"Farewell to The Protestant Ethic?" *Telos*, no. 78 (1988): 81–94.

Oatley, Keith. *Emotions: A Brief History*. Oxford, UK: Blackwell, 2004.

Oatley, Keith, and Elaine Duncan. "The Experience of Emotions in Everyday Life." *Cognition and Emotions* 8, no.4 (1994): 369–81.

O'Connell, Mark. "Why You Should Read W. G. Sebald." *New Yorker*, December 14, 2011. www.newyorker.com/books/page-turner/why-youshould-read-w-g-sebald.

O'Higgins, James, and Michel Foucault. "Sexual Choice, Sexual Act: An Interview with Michel Foucault." *Salmagundi* 58/59, (1984): 10–24.

Oklahoma City National Memorial. "Oklahoma City National Memorial." Press kit. OklahomaCityNationalMemorial.org, accessed on April 1, 2016. https:// oklahomacitynationalmemorial.org/press-room/press-kit/

Orsi, Robert. *Thank You Saint Jude*. New Haven, CT: Yale University Press, 1996.

Parker. A., M. Russo, D. Somner, and P. Yaeger. *Nationalisms and Sexualities*. New York: Routledge, 1992.

Parkinson, Brian, Agneta Fischer, and A. S. R. Manstead. *Emotion in Social Relations: Cultural, Group, and Interpersonal Processes*. Philadelphia, PA: Psychology Press, 2005.

Parkinson, Brian and Antony S. R. Manstead. "Current Emotion Research in Social Psychology: Thinking about Emotions and Other People." *Emotion Review* 7, no. 4 (2015): 371–80.

Percy, Walker. "Symbol, Consciousness, and Intersubjectivity." *Journal of Philosophy* 5 (1958): 631–41.

Perinbanayagam, R.S. *The Karmic Theater*. Amherst: University of Massachusetts Press, 1982.

Signifying Acts. Carbondale: Southern Illinois University Press, 1985.

"Signifying Emotions." *The Sociology of Emotions: Original Essays and Research Papers* 9 (1989): 73.

Discursive Acts. Hawthorne, NY: Aldine de Gruyter, 1991.

The Presence of Self. Rowman and Littlefield, 2000.

"Emotions in Discourse." In *Discursive Acts: Language, Signs, and Selves*, 2nd ed., 167–98. New Brunswick, NJ: Transaction, 2011.

"The Play of Emotions." In *Varieties of the Gaming Experience*, edited by R. S. Perinbanayagam, 43–73. New Brunswick, CT: Transaction, 2015.

Perinbanayagam, R. S. and E. Doyle McCarthy. "Interactions and the Drama of Engagement." *Studies in Symbolic Interaction: A Research Bi-Annual*, edited by Norman K. Denzin 39 (2012a): 121–224.

"Interactions and the Drama of Engagement." In *Identity's Moments: The Self in Action and Interaction*, edited by R. S. Perinbanayagam, 77–107. Lantham, MD: Lexington Books, 2012b.

Peterson, Richard A. "The Production of Culture: A Prolegomenonin." In *The Production of Culture*, edited by R. A. Peterson, 7–22. Beverly Hills, CA: Sage, 1976.

"Cultural Studies through the Production Perspective: Progress and Prospects." In *The Sociology of Culture*, edited by D. Crane, 191–220. Cambridge, MA: Blackwell, 1994.

"In Search of Authenticity." *Journal of Management Studies* 42, no.5 (2005): 1083–98.

Plummer, Ken. *Telling Sexual Stories*. New York: Routledge, 1995.

Polanyi, Karl. *The Great Transformation: The Political and Economic Origins of Our Time*. Boston, MA: Beacon Press, [1944] 2001.

Rabinow, Paul and George E. Marcus, with James D. Faubion and Tobias Rees. *Designs for an Anthropology of the Contemporary*. Durham, NC: Duke University Press, 2008.

Rabinow, Paul and William Sullivan. *Interpretive Social Sciences: A Second Look*. Berkeley: University of California Press, [1979] 1987.

Rabinow, Paul, and Anthony Stavrianakis. *Demands of the Day: On the Logic of Anthropological Inquiry*. Chicago: University of Chicago Press, 2013.

Reddy, William M. *The Invisible Code: Honor and Sentiment in Post-revolutionary France, 1815–1848*, Berkeley: University of California Press, 1997.

The Navigation of Feeling. New York: Cambridge University Press, 2001.

Reed, Isaac A. and Jeffrey C. Alexander. *Meaning and Method: The Cultural Approach to Sociology*. New York: Routledge, 2009.

Revel Foundry. "Welcome to the Age of Experience." Revelfoundry.com, accessed on January 10, 2015. http://revelfoundry.com/welcome-to-the-age-of-experience-infographic/.

Revlin, Andrew C. "The Root of Pope Francis's Appeal among Secular Scientists." *New York Times*, September 26, 2015. http://dotearth.blogs.nytimes.com/20 15/09/26/the-root-of-pope-franciss-appeal-among-secular-sustainability-see kers/?_r=0.

Ricoeur, Paul. *Lectures on Ideology and Utopia*. New York: Columbia University Press, 1986.

Riesman, David, with Nathan Glazer and Renel Denney. *The Lonely Crowd*. New Haven, CT: Yale University Press, 1950.

Ritzer, George. *Enchanting a Disenchanted World: Revolutionizing the Means of Consumption*. 2nd ed. Thousand Oaks, CA: Sage Publications, 2004.

Robertson, Roland. *Globalization: Social Theory and Global Culture*. Newbury Park, CA: Sage, 1992.

Robinson, Andrew. "Art, Aura, and Authenticity." *Ceasefire*, June 14, 2013. https://ceasefiremagazine.co.uk/walter-benjamin-art-aura-authenticity/.

Robinson, David. *Chaplin: His Life and Art*. New York: McGraw Hill, 1985.

Robinson, Paul. *The Modernization of Sex: Havelock Ellis, Alfred Kinsey, William Masters, and Virginia Johnson*. New York: Harper and Row, 1976.

Roche, Maurice. *Mega-events and Modernity*. New York: Routledge, 2000.

Rojek, Chris. *Decentring Leisure: Rethinking Leisure Theory*. Thousand Oaks, CA: Sage, 1995.

Rorty, A. O. *Explaining Emotions*. Berkeley: University of California Press, 1980.

Rosenblatt, Roger. "How We Remember." *Time* 26 (May 29, 2000): 28–30.

Rosenwein, Barbara H. "Worrying about Emotions in History." *The American Historical Review* (June 2002). http://historycooperative.press.uiuc.edu/jo urnals/ahr/107.3/ah0302000821.html.

Rothstein, Edward. "Anecdotal Evidence of Homesick Mankind." *New York Times*, July 20, 2006.

Rousseau, Jean-Jacques. *The Social Contract*. Translation and introduction by Maurice Cranston. New York: Penguin, 1968.

 Émile, or On Education. Translation, introduction, and notes by Allan Bloom. New York: Basic Books, 1970.

Sahlins, Marshall. *Culture and Practical Reason*. Chicago: University of Chicago Press, 1976.

Said, Edward W. *The World, the Text, and the Critic*. Cambridge, MA: Harvard University Press, 1983.

Sartre, Jean-Paul. *The Emotions: Outline of a Theory*. Translated by Bernard Frechtman. New York: Philosophical Library, 1948.

Schechner, Richard. *Performance Theory*. London: Routledge Library, 2003.

Scheff, Thomas J. *Catharsis in Healing, Ritual, and Drama*. Berkeley: University of California Press, 1979.

 "Towards Integration in the Social Psychology of Emotions." *Annual Review of Sociology* 9 (1983): 333–54.

 Microsociology: Discourse, Emotion, and Social Structure. Chicago: University of Chicago Press, 1990.

 Bloody Revenge: Emotions, Nationalism, and War. Boulder, CO: Westview, 1994.

 "Politics of Hidden Emotions: Responses to a War Memorial." *Peace and Conflict: Journal of Peace Psychology* 13, no. 2 (2007): 1–9.

 What's Love Got to Do with It? Emotions and Relationships in Popular Songs. Boulder, CO: Paradigm, 2011.

 "A Wake on the Pier: A Poem." Essay #39, accessed on August 27, 2015, www .soc.ucsb.edu/faculty/scheff.

Scheff, Thomas J. and Suzanne M. Retzinger. *Emotions and Violence*. Lexington, MA: D. C. Health, 1991.

Scheler, Max. *The Nature of Sympathy*. London: Routledge and Kegan Paul, [1954] 1970.

 On Feeling, Knowing, and Valuing. Edited by H. J. Bershady. Chicago: University of Chicago Press, 1992.

Schickel, Richard. *Intimate Strangers: The Culture of Celebrity.* New York: Fromm, 1986.

Schneewind, J. B. "The Use of Autonomy in Ethical Theory." In *Reconstructing Individualism: Autonomy, Individuality, and the Self in Western Thought*, edited by T.C. Heller, 64–75. Stanford, CA: Stanford University Press, 1986.

The Invention of Autonomy. Cambridge, UK: Cambridge University Press, 1998.

Schutz, Alfred and Thomas Luckmann. *The Structures of the Life-World.* Evanston, IL: Northwestern University Press, 1973.

Schweder, R. A. and R. A. Levine. *Culture Theory: Essays on Mind, Self, and Emotions.* New York: Cambridge, 1984.

Sebald, W. G. *Austerlitz.* Translated by Anthea Bell. New York: Random House, 2001.

Sennett, Richard. *The Fall of Public Man.* New York: Knopf, 1977.

Sewell, William H. "The Concept(s) of Culture." In *Beyond the Cultural Turn*, edited by V.E. Bonnell and L. Hunt, 35–61. Berkeley: University of California Press, 1999.

Shalin, Dmitri N. "Pragmatism and Social Interactionism." *American Sociological Review* (1986): 9–29.

Shott, Susan. "Emotion and Social Life: A Symbolic Interactionist Analysis." *American Journal of Sociology* (1979) 13: 1317–34.

Shotter, J. and K. J. Gergen. *Texts of Identity.* Newbury Park, CA: Sage, 1989.

Siegel, Lee. "Cultural Studies: On Celebrities Good and Bad, or Alec Baldwin," Styles. *New York Times*, July 1, 2012.

Small, Albion. "The Meaning of the Social Movement." *American Journal of Sociology* 3, no. 3 (1897): 340–54.

Smith, Laurajane. "Theorizing Museum and Heritage Visiting. In *International Handbooks of Museum Studies*, edited by Andrea Witcomb and Kylie Message. New York: John Wiley, 2006.

Society for the Propagation of the Faith. *Shower of Roses upon the Missions: Spiritual and Temporal Favors Obtained through the Intercession of Blessed Teresa, the Little Sister of the Missionaries.* New York: Society for the Propagation of the Faith, 1924.

Solomon, Robert C. *The Passions.* NY: Doubleday, 1976.

"Getting Angry: The Jamesian Theory of Emotion in Anthropology." In *Culture Theory: Essays on Mind, Self, and Emotion*, edited by R.A. Shweder and R.A. LeVine, 238–56. New York: Cambridge, 1984.

Love: Emotion, Myth, and Metaphor. Buffalo, NY: Prometheus Books, 1990.

"Beyond Ontology: Ideation, Phenomenology, and the Cross Cultural Study of Emotion." *Journal for the Theory of Social Behaviour* 27, no. 2–3 (1997): 289–303.

Thinking about Feeling. New York: Oxford University Press, 2004.

Somers, Margaret. R. and Gloria D. Gibson. "Reclaiming the Epistemological "Other": Narrative and the Social Construction of Identity." In *Social Theory and the Politics of Identity*, edited by Craig Calhoun, 37–100. Cambridge, MA: Blackwell, 1994.

Spender, Stephen. *The Struggle of the Modern.* London: Hamish Hamilton, 1963.

Stark, Werner. *Safeguards of the Social Bond: Custom and Law.* Vol. 3 of *The Social Bond: An Investigation into the Bases of Law-Abidingness.* New York: Fordham University Press, 1980.

Staske, Shirley A. "Talking Feelings: The Collaborative Construction of Emotion in Talk between Close Relational Partners." *Symbolic Interaction* 19, no. 2 (1996): 111–35.

Stearns, Carol Z. and Peter N. Stearns. *Anger: The Struggle for Emotional Control.* Chicago: University of Chicago Press, 1986.

Stearns, Peter N. *American Cool: Constructing a Twentieth-Century Emotional Style.* New York: New York University Press, 1994.

Battleground of Desire: The Struggle for Self-Control in Modern America. New York: New York University Press, 1999.

Anxious Parents: A History of Modern Childrearing. New York: New York University Press, 2004.

Growing Up: The History of Childhood in Global Context. Waco, TX: Baylor University Press, 2005.

Revolutions in Sorrow: The American Experience of Death in Global Perspective. London: Taylor and Francis, 2007.

"Anger Management, American-Style: A Work in Progress." *Hedgehog Review*: (Spring 2010): 8–17.

Stearns, Peter N. and Jan Lewis. *An Emotional History of the United States.* New York: New York University Press, 1998.

Stearns, Peter N. and Deborah C. Stearns. "Historical Issues in Emotions Research: Causation and Timing," In *Social Perspectives on Emotion*, vol. 2, edited by W. M. Wentworth and J. Ryan, 239–66. Greenwich, CT: JAI Press, 1994.

Susman, Warren. *Culture as History: The Transformation of American Society in the Twentieth Century.* New York: Pantheon, 1984.

Swaan, Abram de. *The Management of Normality: Critical Essays in Health and Welfare.* New York: Routledge, 1990.

"Widening Circles of Identification: Emotional Concerns in Sociogenetic Perspective." Presentation at the 1992 Annual Meeting of the International Society for Research on Emotions, Carnegie Mellon University. Published in 1997 as "Widening Circles of Disidentification: On the Psycho- and Sociogenesis of the Hatred of Distant Strangers, Reflections on Rwanda." *Theory, Culture, and Society* 14, no.2 (May 1997): 105–22.

"On the Sociogenesis of the Psychoanalytic Setting." In *Human Figurations: Essays for Norbert Elias*, edited by Peter Reinhart Gleichmann, Johan Goudsblom and Hermann Korte, 318–413. Amsterdam: Stichting Amsterdams Sociologisch Tijdschrift, 2003.

The Killing Compartments: The Mentality of Mass Murder. New Haven, CT.: Yale University Press, 2015.

Swanson, Guy E. "On the Motives and Motivation of Selves." *The Sociology of Emotions*, edited by D.D. Franks and E.D. McCarthy, 3–32. Greenwich, CT: JAI Press, 1989.

Swart, K. W. 1962. "'Individualism' in the Mid-Nineteenth Century (1826–1860). *Journal of the History of Ideas* XXIII (1962): 77–90.

Swidler, Ann. *Talk of Love*. Chicago: University of Chicago Press, 2001.

Swidler, Ann. and J. Arditi, "The New Sociology of Knowledge." *Annual Review of Sociology*, 20 (1994): 305–29.

Taylor, Charles. *Sources of the Self*. Cambridge, MA: Harvard University Press, 1989.

The Ethics of Authenticity. Cambridge, MA: Harvard University Press, 1991.

Modern Social Imaginaries. Durham, NC: Duke University Press, 2004.

A Secular Age. Cambridge, MA: Belknap Press, 2007.

Thoits, Peggy A. "Self-Labeling Processes in Mental Illness: The Role of Emotional Deviance." *American Journal of Sociology* 92 (1985):221–49.

"The Sociology of Emotions." *Annual Review of Sociology* 15 (1989): 317–42.

"Emotional Deviance." In *Research Agendas in the Sociology of Emotions*, edited by T.D. Kemper, 190–203. Albany, NY: State University of New York Press, 1990.

"Managing the Emotions of Others." *Symbolic Interaction* 19, no.2 (1996): 85–109.

"Emotion Norms, Emotion Work, and Social Order." In *Feelings and Emotions*, edited by A.S. Manstead, N. Frijda, and A. Fischer, 359–78. New York: Cambridge University Press, 2004.

Thérèse of Lisieux. *Her Autobiography and Letters*. Translated by T. N. Taylor. New York: P. J. Kenedy, [1898] 1926.

Thompson, E. P. *The Romantics: England in a Revolutionary Age*. Foreword by Dorothy Thompson. New York: New Press, 1997.

Thompson, John B. *The Media and Modernity: A Social Theory of the Media.* Stanford, CA: Stanford University Press, 1995.

Tilly, Charles. *Popular Contention in Great Britain, 1758–1834.* Cambridge, MA: Harvard University Press, 1994.

   Social Movements, 1768–2004. Boulder, CO: Paradigm, 2004.

Tocqueville, Alexis de. *Democracy in America.* Vol. 2. New York: Vintage, [1840] 1990.

Trilling, Lionel. *Sincerity and Authenticity.* Cambridge, MA: Harvard University Press, 1971.

Turkle, Sherry. *Life on the Screen: Identity in the Age of the Internet.* New York: Simon and Schuster, 1995.

   Alone Together: Why We Expect More from Technology and Less from Each Other. New York: Basic Books, 2011.

   Reclaiming Conversation: The Power of Talk in a Digital Age. New York: Penguin Press, 2015.

Turner, Ralph H. "Is There a Quest for Identity?" *The Sociological Quarterly* 16 (Spring 1975): 148–61.

Turner, Victor. *The Anthropology of Performance.* New York: PAJ Publications, 1988.

Turner, Jonathan H., and Jan E. Stets. *The Sociology of Emotions.* New York: Cambridge University Press, 2005.

van Brakel, Jaap. "Emotions: A Cross-cultural Perspective on Forms of Life." *Social Perspectives on Emotion* 2, (1994): 179–238.

Vannini, Phillip and Patrick Williams. *Authenticity in Culture, Self, and Society.* London: Ashgate. 2009.

von Scheve, Christian and Sven Ismer. "Towards a Theory of Collective Emotions." *Emotion Review* 1, no. 1 (May 2013): 1–8.

von Scheve and Mikko Salmela. *Collective Emotions.* New York: Oxford University Press, 2014.

Wagner, Roy. *The Invention of Culture.* Rev. ed. Chicago: University of Chicago Press, 1981.

Wagner-Pacifici, Robin and Barry Schwartz. "The Vietnam Veterans Memorial: Commemorating a Difficult Past." *American Journal of Sociology* 97 (1991): 376–420.

Ware, Sue Anne. "Anti-Memorials and the Art of Forgetting." *Public History Review* (2008):1–78.

Washington, Peter. *Madame Blavatsky's Baboon: A History of the Mystics, Mediums, and Misfits Who Brought Spiritualism to America.* London, UK: Martin Secker and Warburg, 1993.

Weaver, Courtney. *Unzipped: What Happens When Friends Talk about Sex.* New York: Doubleday, 1999.

Weinberg, Darin. "The Enactment and Appraisal of Authenticity in a Skid Row Therapeutic Community." *Symbolic Interaction* 19, no.2 (1996): 137–62.

Wieseltier, Leon. "A Year Later," Washington Diarist. *New Republic*, no. 2 (2002): 38.

Wiley, Norbert. *The Semiotic Self.* Chicago: University of Chicago Press, 1994.

Williams, Raymond. *Culture and Society, 1780–1950.* New York: Columbia University Press, [1958] 1983.

The Long Revolution. New York: Harper Torchbooks, 1961.

"Drama in a Dramatised Society." In *Raymond Williams on Television*, edited by A. O'Connor, 3–5. Toronto: Between the Lines, [1974] 1989.

Keywords: A Vocabulary of Culture and Society. Rev. ed. New York: Oxford University Press. [1976] 1985.

The Sociology of Culture. New York: Schocken, 1981.

"The Masses." In *The Raymond Williams Reader*, edited by John Higgins, 42–64. Oxford, UK: Blackwell, 2001.

Williams, Simon. *Emotion and Social Theory.* London: Routledge, 2001.

Wilson, Catherine. "Vicariousness and Authenticity." In *The Robot in the Garden: Telerobotics and Telepistemology in the Age of the Internet*, edited by Ken Goldberg, 64–89. Cambridge, MA: MIT Press, 2000.

Woody, Robert H. "Music Made for Peak Perception." *Psychology Today*, April 11, 2012. https://www.psychologytoday.com/blog/live-in-concert/201204/music-made-peak-perception.

Woolf, Virginia. "Mr. Bennett and Mrs. Brown." In *The Virginia Woolf Reader*, edited by Mitchell A. Leaska, 192–212. New York: Harcourt, [1924] 1984.

Wouters, Cas. *Informalization: Manners and Emotions since 1890.* London: Sage, 1992.

Wrathall, Mark and Jeff Malpas, eds. *Heidegger, Authenticity, and Modernity.* Cambridge, MA: MIT Press, 2000.

Wuthnow, Robert. *Meaning and Order: Explorations in Cultural Analysis.* Berkeley: University of California Press, 1987.

Young, James E. *The Texture of Memory.* New Haven, CT: Yale University Press, 1993.

"Memory and Counter Memory." *Harvard Design Magazine* (Fall 1999): 1–10.

Zaretsky, Eli. *Secrets of the Soul.* New York: Knopf, 2004.

Zurcher, Louis A. *The Mutable Self: A Self Concept for Social Change.* Berkeley Hills, CA: Sage, 1977.

Index

IRONY

Lightning Source UK Ltd.
Milton Keynes UK
UKOW03n0711310517
302369UK00005B/31/P